Selected Poems: 1970-2005

SELECTED POEMS: 1970-2005

FLOYD SKLOOT

TUPELO PRESS

Selected Poems: 1970-2005
Copyright © 2007 Floyd Skloot
ISBN: 978-1-932195-59-0
Printed in USA. All rights reserved.
No part of this book may be reproduced without
the permission of the publisher.

First paperback edition April 2008
Library of Congress Control Number: 2007941540
Tupelo Press, Inc.
PO Box 539, Dorset, Vermont 05251
802.366.8185
tupelopress.org

Cover and text designed by William Kuch, WK Graphic Design
Cover Painting "Pond Reflections, Giverny" by
Beverly Hallberg (beverlyhallberg.com)

Tupelo Press is an award-winning independent literary press that publishes fine fiction,
non-fiction and poetry in books that are as much a joy to hold as they are to read.

Tupelo Press is a registered 501(c)3 non-profit organization and relies on donations to
carry out its mission of publishing extraordinary work that may be outside the realm of
the large commercial publisher.

For Beverly

Acknowledgments

These poems were selected from the following volumes:

Music Appreciation (University Press of Florida, 1994)
The Evening Light (Story Line Press, 2001)
The Fiddler's Trance (Bucknell University Press, 2001)
Approximately Paradise (Tupelo Press, 2005)
The End of Dreams (Louisiana State University Press, 2006)

Author's Note

Music Appreciation, my first full-length collection, contained poems written between 1970 and 1992.

The Evening Light was completed in 1997 and accepted for publication in 1998, more than three years before it appeared in print. *The Fiddler's Trance* was completed in 2000, barely a year before it appeared in print. So although the books were published within a few months of each other in 2001, three years separated their completion.

The End of Dreams was accepted for publication in 2002, four years before it appeared in print. It was my fourth collection, but appeared a year after my fifth, *Approximately Paradise*. In organizing this volume of selected poems, I have restored *The End of Dreams* to its proper chronological place.

Contents

Acknowledgments and Author's Note

I *from* Music Appreciation

II *from* The Evening Light

III *from* The Fiddler's Trance

I *from* Music Appreciation

TWILIGHT TIME

The Platters, Spring 1958

It could only be
a dream since the drapes
are tied back, there is lilac
sunset above rooftops, and Sabbath
candles flicker in their saucers
just for play. How else
could there be rhythm
and blues on the Victrola
at dusk? My mother softly
sets the needle arm down
and turns to smile at him
through the static, spreading
her feathered boa like angels'
wings before gliding
into my father's arms.

His easy chair has floated
away, the sea of carpet
has parted, and oak dark
as the earth's heart holds
them. I know it is only
in dreams that their hands
touch and twine, that shades
of night would bring them
together like this.
All that is impossible
is that it could have happened.

They move to the smooth blend
of the singers' voices, love
is in their eyes, their separate
days are given up to a mellow
music. Now they are twirling,
together at last at twilight time.

WILD LIGHT

Wild rice is
watergrass
Indians gather at
lakeborders
in northern Minnesota.

Similarly, wild
orange is the laurel
cherry, its flowers
milky white, the fruit
black and sleek.

With its rose
colored cluster of flowers
loose to breeze,
the wild hollyhock is
checkerbloom.
Yes,
and the rooting
stems that creep must
mean wild sweet William
is blue phlox.

You can see wild
carrot is Queen Anne's lace,
the broad umbels of white
flowers like a plum
stained linen on the field,
and the white wild
pink is moss campion.

Wild tomato
is the bloodberry

as wild rocket is
hedge mustard as wild
rosemary is crystal tea

and as I
once
entered the wild light
and named it love.

MY DAUGHTER CONSIDERS HER BODY

She examines her hand, fingers spread wide.
Seated, she bends over her crossed legs
to search for specks or scars and cannot hide
her awe when any mark is found. She begs
me to look, twisting before her mirror,
at some tiny bruise on her hucklebone.
Barely awake, she studies creases her
arm developed as she slept. She has grown
entranced with blemish, begun to know
her body's facility for being
flawed. She does not trust its will to grow
whole again, but may learn that too, freeing
herself to accept the body's deep thirst
for risk. Learning to touch her wounds comes first.

SEPTEMBER FRUIT

This autumn my daughter discovered plums.
She found pineapples, figs, and blackberries,
learned to savor the pleasure that comes
from such summer fruit as sour cherries
in late September. I saw her eyes turn
inward, closing round a vision of lush
casaba. Soon she grew her thick auburn
hair longer. She began to love the hush

of held breath as her body welcomed new
tastes, risking flame tokays and tangerines.
I saw there was little for me to do
but stock apples and pears too. At fifteen,
she felt the world become hers to harvest,
welcoming each new flavor as though blessed.

IN THE COAST RANGE

The clear-cut where my daughter sits
could be forest again, but not
in my lifetime. There is
no hint of water or new growth,
only bleached chips scattered
among stones. A folded shirt
cushions her from the rubble
into which her bare feet have dug.

She climbed this slope
somewhere in the Coast Range
with friends who know more
about her thoughts than I do.
She leans back on her own
hands for support, looking down,
I imagine, toward the sea.
A breeze stirs her hair
and nothing else.

Beyond her, I see the evergreen
looming on the next ridge.
I see them fade south
until they merge
with the morning sky.

YOU ASKED FOR IT

Show me film clips of William McKinley.
Show me Charles Atlas pulling six autos
down two miles of road. I would like to see
the vault at Fort Knox, chimps with hammertoes,
a man boning chickens while blindfolded.

Show me Ebeye Atoll, near Kwajalein,
worst slum in the Pacific. Show me red
squill being made into rat poison, pain
free surgery as performed in Shansi,
old friends playing poker underwater.

Then show me love as it was meant to be.
Show me an old man and his grown daughter
walking alone near a cranberry bog,
not the Robot Man and his Robot Dog.

BRAIN SCAN

Be still. When the chilling rush of liquid
fills your veins, breathe in. As it turns to heat
deep in your bloodstream, breathe out. The acrid
taste in your mouth is nothing. Meadowsweet
light flushing the stark white walls as you slip
inside the machine means nothing–a short
term shift in blood pressure timed to the drip
of dye. Since the least movement can distort

the image, forget that your cradled head
may reveal a hard secret soon, the kind
of growth you fear. Forget the narrow bed
you're strapped to and the woman, safe behind
leaded glass, who adjusts it by remote
control. What matters now is the subtle
shading of mass, some new darkness afloat
in the brindled brain-sea. You must be still.

MUSIC APPRECIATION

What am I doing reading
about tone color and quality of sound?
Largo and *grave* blur to *adagio*
and no one I know pronounces timbre
properly. I listen to the oboe
offering contrast to the amber
melody of the violin.
Alone too long this winter
with the mysteries of disease,
some virus my doctors say
is deep but cannot name,
I learn to listen for music. A trombone
slides from brilliant to mellow
while strings quiver. Here the crescendo
to full orchestra. I may never know
what virus this is, what brilliant cell
rewrites the entire score
my body has followed for life, throwing
its symphony into chaos. It's somber,
but I'm learning to appreciate
this new tone, the discordant sound
that accompanies vital change.
I was thinking *vivace,*
but find that recovery runs
at its own tempo, and settle back
simply to hear the way
my being achieves its harmonies.

SAYING WHAT NEEDS TO BE SAID

Brain lesions have left my lexicon scrambled.
Or maybe it is my brain that is scrambled
and lexicon scattered to flecks of brainwhite,
words looming here and there like stars in a white

sky of negative night. If the world's logic
seems skewed, at least my brain has a pure logic
now, a wild crosswired beauty. So I say
broadcast the cremation when I mean to say

microwave the cream of wheat, or say my blood
tests show amnesia, not the more common blood
disorder anemia. I walk into walls
and say I walked into the roof. There are walls

around abstract thoughts I crash into as well.
The mere concept of health has become a well
too deep to reach for words. I feel confusion
like mine can make sense, though. Take the confusion

when I say Xerox the laundry and Xerox
the lawn. Every machine is now a Xerox
machine to me, which is just another way
of saying what needs to be said anyway.

Sick three years, I have learned to look at the bright
side. You can see the darkest trouble as bright.
For example, I don't say everything twice.
I'd hate to be one who said everything twice.

THE PURE TONGUE

This field of sand held summer
bungalows painted sea blue each June,
painted ivory and violet, radiant
before the wear of wind and storm surges.
Our streets were named for months.
We would walk the years until we were gone.

From the boardwalk to land's end
dunes grew and shrank with the seasons.
But here where steam dredges pumped out
marsh and the silt was buried beneath
pavement, where dunes were held flat
under wood brought in by elephants
a century ago, the old hotels
exposed their brick or stucco faces
to the surf. I remember at dusk
big band music drifted on the spray
of August Saturdays, and women
in fur hats strolled arm in arm.

Here the Ferris wheel mimicked
tumbling surf while the whip
cut its figure eights. An arcade
rang with light in a breeze that caked
the back of my ears with salt.
There I played in the superstructure
of a bowling alley that has turned
into this stretch of strand.

I have come back to my city, built
on fickle ground as though its footing
were bedrock, to imagine it returning
to the pure tongue of sand it was

before. Home again becomes a natural
barrier, alive and moving toward land,
able to replace itself with overwash
as the level of the sea slowly rises.

But I know what has ended is
only beginning again. Luxury
living is already for sale here
where all I can see is a fresh
pour of cement the same drab
color as the heart of a wave.

II *from* The Evening Light

ARGENTEUIL, 1874

As summer sun stipples the garden grass,
Monet is watering his roses. Camille sits
in the noon light, chin on hand, white dress
a pillow for young Jean who no longer fits
across her lap. Missing the city, she
is ready to pack right now if only Claude
could tear himself away. But of course he
wants to spend time painting with Edouard,
and Jean, half-asleep, is already talking about
having a picnic tomorrow. It is always
like this. Now Claude has brought his paints out
to sit beside Edouard and work till day's
end. At least he is turned away from her.

She sees what will happen even before
Pierre arrives. There is no wind to stir
the air, no cloud to change the light; what more
could they hope for? These are men who would paint
their wives on death-beds if the light were right.
Camille smiles and shifts Jean so that his weight
is off her thigh. Oh, they will eat fish tonight,
a red mullet or, better still, fresh eel,
only in her dreams. Perhaps they should
eat this hen and cock clucking at their heels.

After the last Salon, of course the men would
need something like this, a slow summer to
paint their hearts out, a blossoming of sheer
joy together. So there is nothing to do
but hold still in the heat and be here
with all one's heart—perhaps a quick flutter
of the fan to keep Jean calm and herself

fresh—as time slows and the men, in utter
concentration, begin to lose themselves

in the closed circle of their art, and Manet
paints the Monets in their garden as Monet
paints a grinning Manet painting the Monets
in their garden and Renoir paints the Monets
in their garden in the summer in Argenteuil.

KOKOSCHKA IN LOVE, 1914

It does not matter how a mountain found
its way into these waves. Perhaps the wind,
perhaps the war. He turns in predawn light
to find Alma's pale arms held as though bound

to the bedposts. Her eyes are giving back
their horde of pure darkness as though the night
were hers for good. He knows those eyes will rend
his flesh unless he paints them closed, the black

buried in swirling seas along with blood
and the morning's first full blue as the ship
their bare bed has become shatters. The lip
of the whirlpool will be gushing with gold

flecks of foam and silver will mark the clouds.
It is the tempest and she is the bride
of the wind fitted now against his side.
He will do it right if he can just hold

himself together long enough, if he
can disentangle himself before she
feels his absence or a chill in the air,
if he can leave her there without a sound.

MANET IN LATE SUMMER

With his eyes closed
the pain is cobalt
blue flaring to brilliant
orange whenever he is
touched. There are no
black edges and no shadows
to it, only this thick
burst of purest color
in a field spread sap
green to the horizon.

All week he has tried
to paint a young woman
on horseback, a bugler,
an Amazon, anything other
than flowers. Sunk to
the chest in warm water,
he nibbles a loaf of rye
bread tainted with ergot
and swears if he could rise
tonight he would slash
his last canvases to rags
with a palette knife.

As his movements shrink
the world grows too great.
All he knows must now be
contained in two clusters
of white lilacs, the cut
flowers flaring like hope

where they rest on black
cloth. His bath has cooled.
Across the room a vase
of pinks and clematis
catches the fading light.

SEURAT ON THE VERNAL EQUINOX, 1891

Seurat died of diphtheria March 29, 1891. He was 31.

In the pointillist painting of Georges Seurat
the precise placement of dots of pure color
forces a viewer's eyes to mix them much as
paint on a palette, thereby demonstrating

art's truly mutual nature. Surrounded
by paint pots, Seurat stands too close to his huge
canvas to see the effect he seeks, but that
does not matter. In fact, it is the essence

of what he has been trying to show! He holds
a half-dozen brushes between his knuckles
or gripped in his teeth, head teeming with theory.
The way light truly is, the way distance works

on a wave, the way the mind lies to the eyes—
if he can only get it right, there will be
a science of art, perception exactly
re-enacted in all its perfect pleasure.

But Seurat is not well. He would like to tell
Signac how close he is to the exquisite
balance at last. He would like to see the look
on Pissarro's face as he is overcome

by amazement. He would like for his mother
to know his child now; she should meet the woman
he has loved and hidden away. He would like
to rest, swallow without pain, breathe with the old

ease. He spreads his fingers to let the brushes
clatter to their rack, plucks one from his mouth, steps
forward. Yellow ocher for the earth. Next comes
a field of green. He thought there would be more time.

VAN GOGH AND TOULOUSE-LAUTREC
ON THE WAY TO PÈRE TANGUY'S

From behind they look like father and son
hurrying down a wintry Paris street.
The one on the right speeds up as the one
on the left doffs his Homburg, stops to greet
all the women, then shambles to rejoin
his lanky partner who casts suspicious
glances left and right. Henri takes a coin
from his pocket; Vincent hurls a vicious
look at the beggar reaching out for it.
He believes the poor need a different kind
of help, something to arouse the spirit.
It has not been long since he tried to find
the light inside a pauper's home himself.

He rubs a hand over the red stubble
of his beard and hair, singing to himself
a crude song he recalls from the rubble
of last night at the swanky cabaret
Henri favors. When the little man sleeps
is anyone's guess. Vincent wants to say
come along, wants to ask why Henri keeps
wasting time if he was in such a rush
to get there. They both need paints and Vincent
hopes old Tanguy will throw in a new brush
or two, and canvas, perhaps some solvent.
After all, Tanguy has seven Van Gogh's
stashed here and there. He would be a damn fool
to cut Vincent off now. Everyone knows
that though Tanguy is soft, he is no fool.

Hissing through his teeth, Vincent turns to see
a flash of sunlight off Henri's pince-nez.

Such a flabby face. He can see Henri's
bulging eyes even from this far away.
Poor man. Then Vincent notices his friend
has burst into crimson and yellow flame!
Nothing he can do. This must be the end
of Paris, a message from God. The same
thing happened outside Eindhoven a year
ago, friends erupting in fire that lit
a broad stand of cypresses. It was clear
to him then and he made the requisite
move in three days. Still, he will need supplies
if he is to capture what he has seen:

Out of fire, a dwarf come stumbling with cries
of joy on his moist lips, with blue and green
streaks weighing down his cheeks. Good Lord, the man
is odd-looking. Suddenly Vincent hears
what this demon is shouting and he can
hardly believe it. Devil! Those are tears,
fading as he nears, and that is laughter
coming from his lips as he gasps *you are
looking wild, my friend. Is someone after
you?* and takes Vincent's arm. It is not fair,
it is the same thing all over again.

He mutters in English, then French, then Dutch,
thinking he must be near flowers, not men.
He must have peace, is that asking too much?
First there must be color, which is the same
thing Henri thinks as he looks up and knows
he must paint Van Gogh's portrait, all the pain
there, the vast hunger, all the rage that shows
itself in planes and shapes that never rest,
that are in motion as he vows to paint
a portrait of his friend Toulouse-Lautrec.

Looking down, Vincent knows he has been seen.
All the folds of Henri's face disappear
and rosy petals blossom from his head,
so delicate in this light, so sheer.
Vincent smiles. Tanguy's shop is just ahead.

ONCOGENE

Before eyes, before eye color, before
fingers, before breath and cry, it was there.
Nothing to be seen or touched, something more
like a current, a stirring of the air.

When he stood by his desk in second grade
muttering through the pledge of allegiance,
it was there. At ten, the first time he played
cello solos before an audience,

it was there. A readiness in the cells,
an occult passion for growth. When he dreamed,
it was there as the secrets a ghost tells
while the wind shifts. In moonlight as it gleamed

through lids half-open in sleep, it was there.
It was there when he ran beside a creek
at first light, taking the sharp winter air
into the soft tissue of lungs grown weak

now, though he is only forty years old,
though he was strong, though it began somewhere
deep in his bones. That day when he was told,
he already knew. It was always there.

BRAIN LESIONS

*Memory is affected in specific ways by damage to
different parts of the brain.*
–Daniel L. Schacter, *Searching for Memory*

I.

She knows the face in the mirror
is a face, but does not know it
is her own. This house she knows
to be a house, and it contains
the glass that contains both the face
that looks back at her and the man
poised beside the woman standing there.

His gnarled fingers are the same shape
as his lips, and his gray hair is wild
from wind when they drove to this place
he calls her home. It is his voice
that tells her who he is: her Edward,
of course, for how could a woman forget
the man she has loved since childhood?

He is moving aside as though pulled
by the hand that never found its way
into the glass. This dress he brought
for her to wear is so old and shapeless.

Now he returns from somewhere just beyond
the glass to produce a slim young woman
whose chin and mouth anyone can tell
are just like his. She settles between
them, staring with the same hazel
eyes as the woman they hold in place
with their gaze while bright light
pours through a window behind them.

II.

The man kneeling by the azaleas
thinks it is time for him to return
to barracks. First he wants to write
a quick letter to his girl up in Maine.
She was sick with a cold the last time
he heard from her. When was that?
Late December, and here it is April
of 'forty-four. Worried that he will
never learn those damn semaphore signals,
that the war will end before he can
return to the front, that his Top
Sergeant drinks too much whiskey,
he rises and turns toward the open
door where his nurse Clyde bellows
about coming inside. Time for dinner
and the news. There are signs of life
on Mars, Clyde says, and President
Clinton is going to see his daughter
dance Swan Lake. Clyde says all
the residents are seated and hands him
a glass of water. He assumes Clyde
meant Harry Truman, though he is
certain Roosevelt is still in office.
About life on Mars he can only laugh.
Orson Welles tried that one back
in 'thirty-eight, just before the war began.
He sits down and takes off his hat,
which says "Los Angeles Dodgers"
and seems a terrible joke.
Brooklyn is his favorite team.

III.

The man who spent a lifetime
writing love songs loves to see
deer walk across the grass
in dawn light. Watching them
from bed, he thinks their legs
must feel glued to the ground
till the moment comes for running,
as though each step required
deep thought. In his brain now
there is nothing approaching
song. He admires the way
a doe's ears twitch in the wind
as she listens for danger,
the way she dips her chest
gracefully down toward the last
autumn flowers by the apiary
and brings Margaret running
from the house. His wife,
he remembers that. But nothing
about her or himself, nothing
of the songs she sings at night
while a fire crackles behind
them as she says it did when he
wrote them for her. He loves her
stories of their charmed life
together, a life full of color
photographs and record albums
that bring nothing back for him.
They lie scattered around him now
like the flowerbeds these deer
leave behind as they flee.

IV.

She smiles at him and says she reads
all the time, simply all the time,
and they cannot get enough books
in the Home to satisfy her needs.
She writes, too, though not as much
nor as well as he does, and has
published a few poems over the years,
here and there, nowhere he would
have heard of. She turns away,
sees the piles of his books and picks
one up, flipping through the pages.

She turns back and her face ignites
with pleasure. She smiles and tells
him she reads all the time, simply
all the time. They cannot get enough
books in the Home to satisfy her needs.
She looks down at the book in her hand
and admits she writes a little herself,
a few poems now and again, published
over the years, nowhere he would
have heard of. She takes two steps
toward the row of seats, notices the book
in her hand, spins around and tells
him she reads all the time simply
all the time. She shows him what
is in her hand and says *See?*

BITTERSWEET NIGHTSHADE

It has been months since I could walk this far.
At noon the fence row thick with bittersweet
nightshade flashes with summer sun. There are
no clouds, no fleeing deer, no swirls of breeze,
nothing I remember from the last time
I was here. Now I lean my cane against
a post, lying back where the long stems climb
and scramble over everything that rests

in their way. I love to see these blue stars.
Their five points bend back to reveal a blunt
golden cone nestled in the heart of leaf
where in this light long shadows run like tears.
The wide yellow berries starting to run
toward red are the exact color of grief.

SELF-PORTRAIT WITH 1911 NY YANKEES CAP

The subtlest approach would be to ignore
the gray wool cap with its halo of air
vents, its navy blue button, monogram,
and bill. The rounded, crownless fit and air
of slapdash speed should also be ignored
so that the grandeur of the monogram
can assert itself. Of course the Yankees
in 1911 were a weak team
best known for hitting triples and stealing
bases. They were a shadow of the teams
that later came to rule baseball, Yankees
teams who began their greatness by stealing
Babe Ruth from the Red Sox January
Third, 1920. Little Birdie Cree
was the kind of player who wore this cap.
Although a true wizard with the bat, Cree
kept getting hurt, and in January
of 1916 relinquished his cap
and flannels for good to settle beside
the Susquehanna and work in machine
parts. Birdie was my size, too small to play
every day. The body is a machine
after all, and must fit its tasks. Besides,
Cree was temperamental, someone who played
hard, I imagine from his statistics,
and did not consider that his body
might give out. Medical science was far
behind where it is now, when the body
seems to yield its secrets and statistics
to tell us with grave certainty how far
we have let ourselves drift from perfect health.
Yet medical science cannot today
explain how a virus that found its way

to my brain six years ago can today
be responsible for my shattered health,
or how my thoughts get lost along the way
whenever I deal with abstract ideas.
In the mirror, the old cap I forgot
I was wearing gives me a new idea
which, as I turn to note it, I forget.

AUTUMN EQUINOX

I feel my body letting go of light
drawn to the wisdom of a harvest moon.
I feel it welcome the lengthening night
like a lover in early afternoon.

My dreams are windfall in a field gone wild.
I gather them through the lengthening night
and when they have all been carefully piled
my body begins letting go of light.

Indian summer to leaf-fall to first frost
the memories that were carefully piled
become the dreams most likely to be lost.
My dreams are windfall in a field gone wild

now that memory has abandoned them,
now that Indian summer, leaf-fall, first frost
have become the same amazing autumn
skein of those dreams most likely to be lost.

I feel my body letting go of light.
I feel it welcome the lengthening night,
the windfall of dreams that have long been lost
to Indian summer, leaf-fall, and first frost.

CHANNEL

In time the fork my life took
as illness changed its course
will wander to the main stream
and there below the long waterfalls
and cataracts I will begin my rush
to the place I was going from the start.
I imagine looking back to see
the silted mass where a huge bend
holds sunlight in a net of evergreen
and the sky unable to bear its own
violet brilliance a moment longer.
Out of shadows where the channel
crumbles comes the raucous sound
a great blue heron makes when startled.
Scent of peppermint rides breezes
from the valley and I catch hints
of current beneath the surface
just as darkness unfurls.
There I imagine what was lost
coming together with what was gained
to pour itself at last into the sea.

CRITICAL CARE

Nothing

not the fall crop
of fat blackberries that dazzle
now where they have hidden all month
from daylong sun
in a quirk of gnarled scrub oak

nor the suddenly gold leaves
dropping
from maples as we cross the creek
bone dry since early June

nor twin fawns in their spots
still too innocent to run
from what danger we pose

prepares us
to come inside
and see you lying there
in a wash of brilliant light
breathing
only when an eggshell blue
bellows drives the air into you

HER GAME

The nightly round of gin
rummy and shot of schnapps.
They both play to win.
The TV, one of their props,
flickers unwatched, the tints
wrong, the sound low.

She is 88. He hints
her mind and wits are slow
now, no match for his. This
is false and he knows it. Another
prop, such banter; it's his
specialty. He calls her "mother"
when he is close to losing,
Rosie when winning. She'll shake
her head and say "choosing
you was a serious mistake."

The time he had fare
left for one only,
she said she did not care
to walk, rode the trolley
home herself, and made
him walk the mile through rain.

She underknocks. Played
perfectly. It's still her game.

TOOMEY'S DINER

Sundays at dawn were whispers and silent
pissing on the inside of the privy bowl.
If belt buckles merely clicked, zippers
crept shut, and the heels of heavy shoes
only thudded together muffled in our hands,
mother slept on as we crept out the door.

Sunday mornings my face seemed to melt
in ripples of chrome circling high stools
at the bar of Toomey's Diner. The air
inside was thick with breath and smokes
as I spun between my father and brother
waiting for our flapjacks all around.
I saw the soles of my feet turned upside
down in the stools' silvery pedestals
and knew enough to spin without a squeak.

So this was the world outside. Red leather
to sit on, red formica edged in chrome
where my elbows fit, red menus studded
with paper clips. Signs said Special Today.
This was the stuff of weekday dreams. A small
jukebox at every table, rice to keep
the salt dry, toothpicks, a great pyramid
of cereal boxes hiding the cook.
Sunday was sizzling grease and apple juice
glowing pink, then blue in the sudden shift
of neon. Sunday laughter gave off such
heat that walls burst with sweat.

When the day came apart, I always had
the relative silence of knives and forks
on plates, the delicate lids of syrup holders

snapping shut, coffee slurped from steaming mugs,
coins on the counter, the sound of our bill
skewered by Toomey as we turned to leave.

VISITING HOUR

We came straight from school,
crossing the island as winds
rose and fell. From half
a mile away the whitecapped
baywater smelled of fuel oil,
marsh grass, and autumn
darkness. Gulls circled
a trawler nudging the dock.
We gathered in an alley
behind the old hospital
where our fathers recovered,
or declined, or lingered
behind the cold panes keeping
them from us. We were too young
and full of dangerous life
to be allowed inside. Stroke,
cancer of the lung, a broken
hip, severed arm, failing heart.
We named our fathers by what held
them there. Clot, stone, spine.
Taking turns to stand on one
another's shoulders, we tapped
on windows as the sun set.
Fathers smiled within the folds
of their faces, waved, lay back
among the pillows. They turned
white before our eyes, became
empty spaces in our lives,
quiet behind glass in their
gleaming ground floor rooms.

MEMORY HARBOR

—No one creates. The artist assembles memories.
Jack B. Yeats

I no longer know what to trust
when the past comes into view
like a harbor and the boat
my father pilots begins to swing
in one great arc toward the sea.
His face catches the grim morning
light and my mother in the window
of a shack turns away from the view,
fading into the dark. But my father
was a poultry butcher in the city
and my mother never rose with morning
light in their whole life together.

Didn't we live by the sea at the end
and didn't we turn away from one another
morning and night? Wasn't our home
the heart of storm, our shore given
over to the wrack of ebb and flow?

I no longer know where to turn
when loss like a gust of wind
swings me back again to open sea,
where the sun that I knew as a smooth
disk rising behind me grows edges
now as it sets, glowing coral
and bittersweet, glowing crimson
and scarlet in the moment it sinks
below the shimmering horizon.

END STAGE

My brother rises from his easy chair,
staggering as the darkness follows him.
The soles of his feet feel nothing at all
but he has learned how to embrace the air
and sway across the rhythm of his heart.

As his movements loosen, time falls apart
till he finds himself braced against the wall.
His steps have shrunken with his sight and there
is little he can follow beyond the dim
edge of hope that leads him down the hall.

His barefoot shuffling is the sound an old
man makes but he will never get that far.
Now he would settle for the bedroom door
and a slight breeze from the open window
that tells him where he is and nothing more.

He enters a shaft of light and turns gold
for a moment, his skin glowing as though
radiant with warmth. Yet he is always cold,
growing paler as the day wanes, and light
no longer makes a difference. At night

when childhood is the center of his life,
memories and dreams are the only sight
he has. There is something he wants to know,
he says, something important that we are
missing. I listen, knowing he is right.

NEAR THE END

My mother came to live beside the sea.
She hated the sound of surf, smell of brine,
gulls circling before the window where she
sat all day in a bright rage of sunshine.

Everyone was old. Everyone was slow.
They went to sleep too soon, rose too early,
were content to watch films and play bingo,
chat with staff and kowtow to the surly
young women at the front desk. Everyone
had someone living close enough to come
for visits twice a week. One woman's son
tried to move in though he was much too young.

There was something wrong with the moon and sun.
Her worst time was near the end of each day.
The moon rose, the sun set. She was alone
with darkness, chill, and fog over the bay.

HOP FIELDS IN WINTER

By midsummer, twining hop vines will hide
these wires in a mob of bracts and flowers
that seem to mass in a matter of hours,
filling the dense air with a scent of pine.
But now, strung like harps, the fields sing in winds
raging downvalley. We watch as they pass
over the skin of the swollen river
and leave the impression that nothing lasts.

Brackish water ripples over the banks.
Wind tears into a stand of second growth
oak. In a moment, snow begins, thick flakes
in their smooth quadrille reminding us both
of cherry blossoms in late April let
loose in one great squall. I believe you are
thinking of spring planting as you look west
where the road bends and see the Coast Range clear.

We can feel the air warming. Where the storm
has been, morning light drenches the snowpack
before creeping toward us, nudging the dark
away. The wires wink, shiver, but hold firm.

DAY OF THE RAINBOW

Until everything was rainbow, rainbow, rainbow!
Elizabeth Bishop, *"The Fish"*

The day we drove straight into a rainbow
began with ocean wind and spindrift gone
wild inside Whale Cove. We saw spume glow
as though praising the memory of dawn
and waves charge the early morning air
like a storm front. Across an arc of beach
a couple walked the dark parabola where
bare trunks lay tangled beyond the tide's reach.

We saw swash drench salt-fretted sandstone
till the cliff seemed to shudder, though we knew
it was only wind stroking the grassy backbone
of Depoe Bay. Since there was a shaft of blue
sky like a quill in clouds above the headland,
and light was strong enough to hint those clouds
lacked passion for a storm, we went to stand
where the downwarped land had long ago drowned

a river that once had emptied here.
Above us two herring gulls wheeled back
and began their swoop to scavenge the shore,
heads dusky for winter, white wings tipped black,
bills agape as they rose squealing and still
hungry from the breakers. Even as the sky
absorbed them in its own granite will,
we knew it was another trick of the eye–

if we held our place they would reappear
against the surf in a flash of underbelly.
But more than anything, it was the sheer
force of the gulls' appetite that made us see

the time had come to start our journey home.
From Otis to the Coast Range the Salmon River,
gorged with snowmelt, its center all foam
and silt, raised its voice as though to deliver

a curse on the new year. We guessed we were
mastering the signs since the day we drove
straight into a rainbow the rain itself never
found us. Soon we passed a hazelnut grove
near Grand Ronde and the sky before us burst
into brilliance. The fallow valley would
have been enough to show nothing was cursed,
not when sodden wheat and onion fields could

suddenly imply a dazzle of July
in green and gold at the edge of the eye.
But we had more. We saw a rainbow span
the road. We saw that one end began
in an orchard north of Highway 99,
rising from a cluster of grape vines
like the essence of scent made visible,
and the other began in the hill

that kept our home hidden among scrub oak,
maple and Douglas fir. Despite the cloak
of clouds that blocked the sun, we saw above
us true color could hold fast as we drove,
could endure, and even lead us to our door.
I thought backwards one hour to the shore
surely buried now by storm surge and tide.
I thought ahead, then put my thoughts aside.

SWANS IN GALWAY BAY

Seven pairs of swans preen
this morning near the docks.
We walk down together
searching among the rocks
for a perfect feather
to commemorate the scene.

The swans float, one foot still
tucked underneath a wing,
the other held steady
as a rudder. They seem
both unconcerned and ready
for whatever the day will

bring them as they drift past.
Soon they are swept away
in pairs where the River
Corrib surges into Galway Bay–
from here just a sliver
of jagged slate-blue glass

but fierce enough to spin
them sideways toward the sea.
Paired still, they carry on
their slow ceremonies,
adjusting with utter calm
to the currents they move in,

content, it would appear,
to end up wherever
they find themselves as long
as they are together,
each feather where it belongs,
each mate with a clear

line of sight to the other.
We have come to the docks'
end emptyhanded. I turn
back, but she stops to watch,
holding me there as one
small feather drifts to shore.

SOURWOOD NOCTURNE

August nights the sourwood droops
with creamy white flowers that come
and go as though the dark of fall

were pure illusion. Walking some
nights on a deer trail that loops
the hillside, we can believe all

we hope for is present in one
deep breath. Then a moment
later is September. The slight

sourwood leaves turn such brilliant
scarlet it seems summer sun
still smolders in the tree's heart.

This high the evening light runs
toward December in a large wash
of blues, translucent as time

tightens and the air grows harsh.
Something moves behind us, a summons
within the wind. We turn toward home.

DAYBREAK

The shapes that moved outside
our door tonight were four deer
come to feed on the last winter
weeds. The riot of their flight
seemed to echo through the dark
when I left my bed to see them.

Now the valley sends its voices
up through morning mist. Cows low,
the sheep farmer's old border
collie barks as she herds strays,
and the southbound freight is
an hour late. Where our hillside
plummets, a fringe of feathery
wild grasses webbed with frost
bends as though lost in prayer.

My wife built this house round
because a clear loop of moonlight
found the space for her early
on a morning like this. She woke
in her down sleeping bag under
a canopy of second growth to hear
great horned owls call from oaks
creaking in a sudden surge of wind.
When she sat up, there was a deer
standing exactly where a dowser
had told her the well should go.

FLIGHT

The summer night is flying
by, rattling windows where light
is alive. Bats are shadows,
brilliant flickers in a mist
of insects, and bumblebees
circle the hyssop. The air
thickens. Directly above
us now a small plane crosses
the horizon of the half
moon on its way to the sea.

This is a night even deer
might soar. We believe they are
searching for a wind somewhere
within the thicket of wild
rose, hazel and blackberries.
We believe the dark whisper
of grasses to be an owl's
wing pulse, the drift of oak leaves
an echo of shifting tides
from beyond the Coast Range.

As silence glides in gentle
spirals back to the earth, first
the sheen, then the shock of all
we have seen comes clear. This is
the moment we know pure flight
has little to do with lift
or drag and much to do with
dreams. It is the moment we
turn together to begin
our own powerful ascent.

III *from* The Fiddler's Trance

RASPUTIN IN DARKNESS

After the Naproxen and Neurontin,
    after the Ketoprofin,
the magnesium straight into my veins,
    after Minor Blue Dragon
        and flax seed oil
    chased by low-fat cottage cheese,
        after seven rounds
of acupuncture and a bed cushioned
        by thick Swedish foam,
    a mattress built of magnets,

    after a spell in the place
where tides begin, just beyond the embrace
        of light, a balance
    point where the earth does not spin,

        it was the middle
of the night and I was home,
staring out the window at moonlit oaks,
    when I saw his beard ruffle
        in a swirl of wind.

He wore a black cloth coat corded by rope
    with a hint of crimson silk
        at the throat. A great
golden crucifix sprouted from his breast
        pocket with its chain
    looped across the transverse piece.
He stood on the grass with fingers tangled
        in his hair, nibbling
a sprig of parsley from our herb garden
        and staring into the room.
A ring of icons dangled and glimmered

in the limbs above his head.

I heard the darkness fill with chanted prayers.
        It was possible to see
                him sway as his arms
rose like wings against the faint scaffolding
        of second growth behind him
and his fingers twitched when they reached for God.
                His eyes became stars.
        Then they grew softer than air
                in the still moment
before storm and I knew he wanted to
        lay his healing hands on me.

        He said *You have sent for me*
                and his voice was mist
on the glass that faded as he waited
        for me to open the door.
                All he wanted in return
was Madeira and a few little sweets,
        potatoes boiled in their skins,
a platter of fish, and fat samovar
        bubbling on the credenza.
                He wanted gypsy
music, wild dancing, a woman's laughter
                breathed into his ear.
He wanted my shaky tenor lifted
                in old Jewish songs
        that mourned a life I had lost.
Then he wanted the summer night to be
                long and luminous
        with soft Siberian light.

        My silence rose like a psalm
                on the delicate
tracery of my wife's breath in the bed.

I turned back to her.
Rasputin whispered something to the trees
and then it was dawn,
the hoarse stanzas of western
tanagers mingling to a song of praise
as sunlight suffused
the circle of shadow where he had stood.

THE SECRET LIFE

The women were always dancers
for the Bolshoi. Lean and lithe,
with enormous eyes, flaring tempers
and diamond tiaras in the evening hours,
such women were hard everywhere
their lovers were soft. There was
no cooking, no cleaning.
There were not even afternoons.

The men were always vast
with power, shielded by wealth
and moustaches, given to beef,
to raw spirits. Such men snored
even when they were awake.
There was always snow, wind
whistling through trees, and fog
on every window in the room.

Once in a while shots rang out.
Once in a while the wife showed up,
sobbing against a lintel or great
with rage in the dark backstage.
Once in a while there was a brother
to worry about, consumptive, fierce-eyed,
needing rest on a mountaintop.

Things never ended well. Trains shrouded
in steam, a crisis on the front, sudden
blood. Nothing but the sound of breath
coming and going in the stillness,
the darkness of a new moon, one last
flickering glance at the slowly ebbing tide
as music rose and the plush curtains closed.

SAGE

He loves to see the purple whorls of sage
in bloom, its knee-high woolly branches white
at noon, their stalked green leaves seeming to age
toward gray in the relentless summer light.

From his bed with its garden view he thinks
of bees that feed on sage to make a prized
honey, of sage juice for joint pain. He drinks
sage tea to prevent night sweats and to ease

his trembling, uses a wash of sage to soothe
sore gums and blacken graying hair. Nothing
helps, but he feels there is nothing to lose.
Burnt sage for the room, sage on scabs, smoking

sage cigarettes for his lungs, sage with roast
duck to cut the fat. He does not want to
live forever. What he wants is almost
more than he can say. A year, maybe two.

WILD BLACKBERRIES

—In memory of my brother

In mid-July the blackberries were tart
and firm within their sweet surrounding flesh.
The full day's sun had just begun to mark
itself on the hidden red as a wish
for time, one week more at most, and warm nights
without rain. Thorns, leaves simple and lobed, dew
poised on dark branch tips framing the last white
flowers: everything reminded me of you
at the end, in a thicket of tubes, blood
spun clean for one more day, glistening hair
suddenly gray in a fan around your head.

The solstice brought a drenching rain as light
left summer behind. Berries draped with mold
shriveled to their stems and vines seemed to fold
in on themselves like dreams under the weight
of swarming yellowjackets. Here and there,
especially if my eyes were closed, I caught
a whiff of missing sweetness in the air.

REMISSION

When all my symptoms melt away like ice
that stilled our pond down to its hidden spring,
I find myself, as though a stranger twice
removed from life, believing everything

I see will remain as clear as it seems
in the shock of morning light. I am out
of season, feeling Spring when Fall sun gleams
off frost or an oak leaf with its stem caught

in a strand of spider web writhes before
the pumphouse door in swirling wind. The dark
edge of hope lurks where time springs shut. No more
incandescent visions, only the stark

truth of spring in my legs down a steep trail
and the clear sign of breath when I exhale.

CELESTIAL NORTH

Nights like this you could tell me time
is porous as gauze and I would believe
you. Tell me tonight has always happened
and always will be happening, since nothing
I know any longer says No. Whisper it
and I would believe you. Tonight the breeze
cooling us comes from the place where dreams
are harbored. Say this moment when winter
swivels into spring is genesis writ small,
say light is the center of darkness,
and I would turn toward it like a flower,
following your hand across the heavens
as it finds the north celestial pole.

THE YOGA EXERCISE

Within a rushing stream of morning light
she stands still as a heron with one sole
held flush against the other inner thigh
and her long arms like bony wings folded
back so that when the motion of a breeze
passes through her body there is a deep

repose at its root and in an eye's blink
she has become this gently swaying tree
stirring in the wind of its breath while linked
to ground by the slow flow of energy
that brings her limbs together now in prayer
and blessing for the peace she is finding there.

POPPIES

For years after a blaze, tree poppies
will spread brilliant yellow flowers
like the echo of flames in chaparral.
Camouflaged among crumbling bones of earth,
the pale salmon petals of pygmy poppies
thrive in thin alpine air. I have seen
acres of Oregon rainbows given over
to blind buds in hot southern sunlight,
cream cups tip their teeming bowls under
a sundown wind, and prickly poppies turn
back cattle grazing a north Texas pasture.
I have been where winter rains stitch
a patchwork of Amapola del Campo
on the spring countryside. So I love
the moment your eyes close, when you become
the fire poppy whose buds must droop
before its flushed flowers will open.

SEED

She is alive. Although her doctors said
there was nothing to be done, she is home,
planting her summer garden, is not dead,
and plans to eat everything she has grown
in this plot, each carrot and tomato,
each squash, pepper, lettuce leaf. She will live
beyond the harvest and what will not grow
is her tumor, its flowers held captive
and still beneath her heart. Only the live
wire of her will separates her now from
the future displayed in black and white five
months ago, backlit clearly. It will come
sooner or later, but this is her time
to cultivate and seed. She is alive.

THE FIDDLER'S TRANCE

–after Chagall

The air above Vitebsk was filled with Jews
gassed green. From the synagogues and orchards,
rubble of butcher shops, from crushed forges,
charred barns, and wooden huts rose the blues
and blazing yellows of the world to come.
Red footprints racing nowhere across snow
were chased by spirals of dark fire that no
one saw in time. Every bird was struck dumb
by dawn. Chagall remembered the future
before ever leaving home. Yet he knew
song was possible. Whatever was true
about the sound of night, he would picture
one lonely fiddler looming and entranced
to find himself the center of a dance.

THE TSAR AT DAWN

The sound that wakes me is a doe leading
　　　　　her two fawns through the mantle
of oak and maple leaves shrouding my yard.
　　　　　　　　I turn to see her
freeze, then flee through a crease of dripping fir
　　　　　with her young leaping after–

and into a shaft of brilliant sunlight
　　　　　walks Nicholas, head down, hands
clasped behind his back, hunting for mushrooms.
　　　　　He stops to stretch his shoulders
　　　　　　　　and neck as though just
　　　　　awake from the deepest sleep.
　　　　　　　　The man loves nothing
so much as such mornings after hard rain,
　　　　　dew glistening on the grass,
　　　　　　　　undulating lines
　　　　　of honking Canada geese
　　　　　　　　passing overhead,
and the rash salute of mushrooms at dawn.

　　　　　He does not know where he is,
or where his guard of Don Cossacks has gone,
　　　　　　　　or why the weather
is so mild for this time of year, no snow
　　　　　　　　so far into fall,
　　　　　or even that I lie here
　　　　　　　　while my fever spikes
watching him bend to inspect a circle
　　　　　of creamy white fairy rings.

He has been haunting the woods
all week. The blue of his eyes is a dream
                 of clear winter skies
softening to the shade of solstice prayers
                 as the day drags on,
         then lakewater in mountain
craters or the flowers of Russian sage
         where he has stopped now to kneel.
                 Those shut umbrellas
are shaggy manes, best if gathered when young.

You can see he is a man who welcomes
                 time alone. Last night, when trees
                 swaying in the wind
set off the motion sensors, I wondered
                 at first if it was
his wandering that filled the night with light,
         if it was his voice I heard
keening somewhere in the middle distance
         for his wife and five children
lost forever in a summery flash.

He rises again, a ragged darkness
         at the knees of his trousers,
and finds himself drawn to a bright cluster
         of puffballs where the land dips
down to our abandoned apiary.
         From behind, he looks younger
than I am, straight-backed and thick in the trunk,
         a man with time on his hands.
I remember moving like that nine years
ago, before the first signs of illness.

                 Perhaps he has come
         to take me away with him,
                 returning me to

a place beyond the Pale of Settlement.
                    Perhaps he has come
            to teach me that I must love
                    him, though he never
            meant my people anything
but harm. He may have come for nothing more
            than to linger in these woods
                    that have been helping
me heal. The kid leather of the puffball's
            mass draws him down, makes him smile
as he reaches out to stroke its smooth white
            flesh in search of the tell-tale
                    cracks and yellow tinge
that would be the first signs of bitterness.

BEHIND GERSHWIN'S EYES

They did not believe him.
They told him the smell
of burning garbage was all
in his head. Some mornings
it was all he could do
to lift his head from
the pillow. Some nights
his brain was on fire,
songs he thought would take
a hundred years to write
suddenly aflame behind
his bulging eyes.

Dizzy in the barber's
chair, dizzy before
the chorus, dizzy
on the tennis court.

They did not believe him
even when he was adrift
in the first movement
of his Concerto in F.
He felt darkness beyond
the footlights seep
into his soul, nothing
but a sea of dream
everywhere, and heard
the echo of unplucked
strings, a quiver
of timpani dying out
quickly as one long
note from an oboe
wafted heavenward.

Then he found himself
back in Los Angeles,
familiar body still
upright on the piano stool,
Smallens with his baton
frozen at the shoulder,
only to blunder again
in the *andante,* and they
told him nothing was wrong.

Dizzy in the Brown
Derby, dizzy before
the surf, dizzy
in the swimming pool.

They believed he was
not happy in Hollywood.
There is nothing wrong
with Gershwin that a song
hit wouldn't cure.
It was in his head, he was
lovelorn or he was riddled
with guilt, he was balding
and drooling, muddle-headed
by noon, listless underneath
the stars. They believed
him sapped by motion picture
making, and longing for New
York City. Those hands
once a blur on the keyboard
could only move slow as flowers
toward the sun yet nothing
was wrong. In the spring
those sandaled feet
that could only shuffle
in the summer garden

had been quick as flame
to his own new music
yet nothing was wrong.

A blade of light
where the drawn shades
meet. Roses without odor,
icewater leaping from its cut
glass goblet, eyes leached
of luster in the shadowy
mirror of his brother's eyes.
He spread chocolates melted
in the oven of his palm
up his arms like an ointment,
and soon he was gone.

RAVEL AT SWIM

The inability to communicate speech, writing or music when the peripheral
nervous system is largely undamaged is called an aphasia.
–John O'Shea, "Maurice Ravel:
Aspects of Musical Perception"

Something dark has stolen the sea from me.
Always a seal in water, I found its
melodies and swam open harmony
through them. Now I flail. Nothing I do fits

the rhythms around me. *Swiss Watchmaker*
they called me for the design of my work.
Mere lover of wind-up toys, a baker
of sweets, as though elegance were a quirk.

Now the hand that holds forks by their tines floats
like driftwood on the sea of music spread
before me. It will not copy the notes
I hear like a gulls' bent tones in my head.

It will not play what I see on paper
and know I wrote two years ago to be
performed one-handed. That was a caper!
I loved having such limits placed on me.

It will not sign my name. It tries to light
a match with the tip of a cigarette.
What is left? It took me eight days to write
a fifty-six word letter I have yet

to end, consoling a friend whose mother
just died. I do not want to be seen now
by anyone who knew me at another
time. Pure artifice, they said, missing how

my need for form affirmed the passions of
my heart. They must not see me with the link
from brain to limb severed and all I love
lost. Sheer formlessness surrounds me. I think

but cannot share my thoughts. I remember
every flower's fragrance, the taste of lamb
roasted for hours over charcoal embers
at summer bazaars, lips on mine, but am

powerless to express myself. Let me
be alone. Let me have the grace of pure
music in my head, where I hear and see
perfectly. That silence I can endure.

STARRY NIGHT

Perhaps I might really recover if I were in the country for a time.
—Vincent Van Gogh

Tonight the moon throbs with light
it seizes from stars as they rise
and the cypresses grow holy
before my eyes. Wind fills the sky.
I see clouds shudder, houses
and shops cower, but somehow
high grass finds its own source
of stillness. I think it is violet
in nature. Never has there
been such a night for seeing
how the dark world thrives
when day's brilliance dies
and sight fully becomes surprise.

Who would want all these deep blues
to soften as though toward dawn?
No dawn will bring along
a day as pure again. Who would
want to be well enough to lose
such hues? I know a man can
be so far from madness the true
world cannot find him. I know
he will be saved only when
the moon collects enough radiance
to render heaven tangible
as the breath of sunflowers.

Look: there is a glow inside
the emptiest spaces when we
study their darknesses. There is
also a hush no stroke of

a painter's brush can muffle.
Think of the instant swallows
rising above a field you enter
suddenly loop back in unison—
a thick landscape of faith
that is beyond words, yet explains
why I am standing here at all.

FREUD IN LONDON, 1939

There is pain in his mouth and jaw,
intimate pain beyond reach of drugs.
He has known it would kill him
since the first signs that distant summer
his grandson died. Torment in the snout
and heart these sixteen years, and nothing
but work to compensate. There is Anna
still unmarried. Adler, Abraham, Ferenczi,
all of them dead and Jung running wild
in the Alps. At night, sirens in the air.
All day, soft voices of farewell in the air.

He thought it would be easier to die.
But there are sons still at large in Germany,
Moses to be explained, and belief in God,
and evil on a scale even he could imagine
in theory only. There is the lure of sleep
and dreams. There is hunger for silence.

He is free but knows he will never recover
from leaving his beloved Vienna behind.
Never recover from the agony in his bones
or the smell that seeps from his wounds.
The dog will no longer come near.
Who can blame him? The flesh melts
as though practicing for death and light
here is never good. The world's borders
are all gone, the Great War settled like ash
on the crotch of history, and the mind
twists around its most secret desire.
Schur with his morphine hovers in the dark.

DELIUS & FENBY

To be a genius, as this man plainly was, and have something beautiful in you
and not be able to rid yourself of it because you could no longer see your
score paper and no longer hold your pen—well, the thought was unbearable!
—Eric Fenby, *Delius As I Knew Him*

Always toward sunset Delius grew
restless and uneasy in his carriage
chair, raving at the pain in his legs,
flicking his long tapering fingers
as though stating a theme on the air.
His proud head, pale as marble,
began to wobble no matter the effort
to hold it still. He demanded a thick
rug for warmth. He demanded a thin rug
for comfort, then demanded that no
rug touch him, all the time wanting
me to read one more story aloud
like a child refusing to go to bed.

Delius required that everything
be just so. His bean and barley
soup must be salted in the pot
and served piping hot. No rattling
cups or clattering spoons at table,
where chitchat lashed him to fury.
After dinner, one cigar and a slow
push up the Marlotte road in silence,
when even the neighbor's great Alsatians
walked hushed beside us. Saturdays
we could play only Sir Thomas Beecham's
records of Delius on the gramophone
in the quiet of his music room.

One morning in the faded garden
where Delius sat beneath the elder
tree, I could see that he was angry
with me. Tossing his head from side
to side, he champed and glared
toward the rising sun, clearing
his throat fortissimo. At night
a melody had come on the verge
of sleep, making him weep to be
hearing new music leap in his mind
again. But I overslept beneath
the full-sized face of mad Strindberg
by Munch, dreaming myself south
to Paris amidst a wild summer storm,
surrounded by young friends in good
health, rain playing a sudden cadenza
on the swollen Somme, and the thunder
in E-Flat. I wanted tea.

My hair still damp, my face creased
by sleep, I took up paper and pen
without a word. I sat cross-legged
on the grass wondering whether Delius
would sing to me. Would he call out
the notes and their time-values?
At last I was to do what I had come
from Scarborough to do and free him
of the music. He threw his head
back like a wild horse in flight
and neighed toneless to the sky.
"Hold it!" he said, causing me
to drop my pen, then he bayed
toward heaven again. I heard
neither words nor notes, only
a shapeless cry. He could not
bring forth the tune he heard!

Dazed, all I could say was
"Delius, what key is it in?"
"A minor, Fenby, don't be slow."

Fingers inky, spectacles blurred
by tears, I confess being blind
as Delius himself when I groped
for the sanctuary of his porch.
Of course, in time we learned
to bring forth his music, imagining
ourselves on cliffs in the heather
looking out over the sea, knowing
chords in the high strings were
a clear sky. But I shall never
forget Delius, a shrunken relic,
mouth opened in anguish, gripped
by the awful beauty inside him .

CURRENTS

The great blue heron rides a cottonwood
limb downriver. She spins through a circle
of sunlight as her mate's wide loops dazzle
the morning and his hoarse squawk says he would
join her if he could. He swoops close to see
again there is no room. She turns her long
neck slower than the limb turns in the strong
current, keeping him in sight as though she
imagines currents of air mimic dark
river currents she will dare when the time
comes. He moves like a dancer past his prime,
a beat slow for her and just off the mark,
but game while she waits against the measure
for a moment they can enter together.

FROST

Wizened, spoiling for a fight, Frost is here
again. I have tried adjusting my pain
medication and sleep schedule, but still
he comes back to wander these woods like wind
stirring the Douglas fir. There is a gleam
of cold light where he stops and squats to track
the cries of naked oak that lean against
a surge of squalls.
                    I hear him rhyming oak
with choke, then smoke and cloak as he looks down
into the valley. It will grow slowly
visible with the lifting of morning
mist and he will allow himself a small
smile. Spoke. Broke.
                        Finally he turns to me,
lifting his chin to indicate the rough
grove at my back. "I see you lost your bees."
I nod as though I always speak with ghosts.
"They were gone before I got here."
                                      Frost first
showed up with late September's heavy rain,
a creature of the equinox, I thought,
till I got a closer look. He follows
his own timetable like the pack of deer
that comes and goes now hunting season has
ended.
          "You need some chickens," he whispers.
"Good layers kept me and mine alive through
lean years." He leads me straight uphill. Baroque.
Folk. Roanoke. "Awoke," I say and he
stops dead to let me know who makes the rules.

Then his face unfolds, thawing as he seems
to grow young before my eyes. "Like your cane,"
he says, and winks when he adds "don't tell me:
Hazel from Rapallo in honor of
Ezra Pound." He shakes his shaggy head. Yoke.
Hoax. "They let him go when I told them to."

Because I have been reading Freud I know
this is the key. First illness, then prison,
then being freed by Frost. Wish-fulfillment,
the heart of every dream. He makes his way
toward a pile of pine and points to the axe.
Stroke. Soak. "Running low." I turn to find him
drifting west with the sun and well beyond
reach of my voice." There is more seasoning
behind the gazebo," I tell thin air
and watch another morning shape itself
around the twist of winter on the wind.

BEE PURPLE

*Bees' eyes can pick up much of what ours can, but in addition they can see a
wavelength of light, a color, impossible for us to perceive.*
                                    –Philip J. Hilts, *Memory's Ghost*

Deep in a montane forest two bees flit
among the sego lilies, seeing dark
purple crosses where all we see are white
petals tinged sometimes with hints of lilac.
In early summer these showy flowers
are bells ringing where the mountain towers
above us and we are deaf to it all.

Perhaps this soil is singing. Perhaps June
ends with scents of lavender and heal-all
even though we cannot smell them, and soon
wind feels exactly like the sea. We call
this sundown. We welcome the full moon
fading to a white we have learned to doubt,

the flash of gray blue pinyon jays whose short
quavering laugh is what ushers us out
of the pines and into the world we thought
we knew. We welcome night. The vast silence
is filling with sound as our still world spins.

CHRISTMAS CHOIR

The smoky contralto sheds her leather
jacket and drapes a scarf around her throat
for warmth, complaining about the weather
while a soprano frets over the note
she could not reach last week. The twin brother
of the choir master hammers out a few
chords of *Limehouse Blues* to get his fingers
loose and refuses to talk to the young
female tenor, one of the best singers
they have found in years, who wrapped her long
legs around him last night but called him Jack
instead of Raymond. Meanwhile another
brother can be heard rehearsing a new
solo in the narthex, his baritone
spilling like December light down the nave.
They noticed he was again dressed in black,
mourning, rumor has it, a dead lover.
One bass and his alto wife will be gone
opening night; both mezzo-sopranos believe
they will miss the same Thursday performance,
since it is the first night of Chanukah,
and the choir master himself is not sure
his wife can sing because there is a chance
the growth on her left tonsil will require
surgery. But here they are together
on the chancel, coughing and murmuring,
their voices warm now, coming together,
rising and falling, and they begin to sing.

LIME AT THE EDGES

Lime at the edges,
a world washed in citrus light
as though spring
burst
this year on the brink of time.

Something to do with looking
straight
at the source.
Something to do with breaching
the thin sheath
of air, a season given
over to
more heat than ever before.

I do not like being still
this morning
here where the river
bends west, but I must
rest
a while in the gathering
wind.
Where is the belted
kingfisher
hovering over water
like a hummingbird?
Where is the tiger
swallowtail sipping nectar
from the blackberry
vine, or the silver salmon?

I need to see the pale gloss
               of false dawn,
                         hues
          well-known from a life
                    by the sea.
I need something familiar
                              seen
from the corner of my eye,
something the color of faith.

      Lime at the edges
with not even a hint of blue.
          I may have looked
          too long last night
                    at the full
moon in all its glory.

THE LANDSCAPE OF SILENCE

There is a silence thin enough
to pierce the loudest cry. I heard
it first at night within the surf,
a secret of the sea, one word
whispered through breakers like the hiss
of foam. I heard it as the wish

moonlight makes in the folds of waves.
Once I heard it in the center
of a thunderstorm as roof eaves
gave. I felt a fury enter
the heart of my dream, but the still
place held. It was like a deep well

echoing the sound of my breath
long after I had walked away.
Silence called me back to myself,
revealing the edges as day
is revealed in the new moon's light.
And I heard it again tonight

in the winds of County Mayo
as scarlet flowers from the wild
fuchsia poured through my closed window
in a dream. I sat up to find
evening shadows in the middle
of the night. Time is a riddle

they spoke in my ear. Its answer
is shadows and flowers from dreams,
silence in bells of wild fuchsia
pealing around me till it seems
I have grown deaf to all other
sounds but the plainsong of wonder.

DANCING IN THE COSMOS

At first I thought the new
moon was pulling us straight
toward the cosmos in bloom
and singing at your yard's
edge. Then I heard the tune
rising. We began to swirl
in a warm whirlwind, sheer
scarves encircling us
like the scent of snapdragons
and sword lilies all crimson,
pink and yellow where your
hillside buckles valleyward.

A sudden shift in tempo
let us spare the lacy
crowns of fennel bent
to our waists by the weight
of their seeds and left us
meshed in raspberry vines.
One look and again I knew
we would soon be hopelessly
deep in the feathers
and petals of the cosmos.

But I believed the music
filling the night was saying Give
in, spin through the cosmos
with faith we will not harm
even the palest wildflower
with our inspired capers.
I believed because the clear
sky we slept under this summer
was still teeming with wild

harmonies. Bats swooped
to owl shrieks and the Milky
Way soaked up the moon's
last offering of light.
So the land was going dry.
So the sun was hotter than ever.
Such nights, such alien dancing,
and never did we lose
a single frilled floret.

GIFT

This is a spring he never thought to see.
Lean dusky Alaskan geese nibbling grass
seed in his field, early daffodils, three
fawns moving across his lawn in the last
of afternoon light, everything he had
let go with small ceremonies on dark
September nights has suddenly come back.
The taste on his tongue is of tamarind
chutney, fish curry, clove, tangs he adores
above all else. He smells the hyacinth
and can feel hope with the terrible crack
of a thawing river loosen in his heart.
He imagines sailing among the Queen
Charlottes come April, tacking into wind
that is the kindest he has ever known,
then gentle breakers, golden sanded shores.

IV *from* The End of Dreams

A HAND OF CASINO, 1954

My grandfather studies the cards.
His jaw juts and he begins to shift
the pink plate of his false teeth,
tonguing it out and in, mouth
widening till his grin has flipped
upside-down between the gums.
He slams a deuce onto the table.

Even at seven I know he is losing
on purpose. He mumbles deep
in his throat, a gargle of sounds
like someone choking on stones.
I think he would make sense
if his teeth were put in right.

At seven I also know that bodies
crumble but new parts can come
gleaming from dark hiding places.
I have seen, buried at the back
of his top drawer, my father's spare
glass eye in a navy velvet box.
My mother has three heads
of stiff hair inside her closet,
just in case, and a secret pack
of fingernails in her chiffonier.

My grandfather strings phrases
of Polish and Yiddish around words
in French to hold his broken
English together. I understand
nothing he says but everything
that is in his eyes. He tells me
he is *a man from the world.*

That must be where he learned
that losing is winning as a frown
is a smile and a curse is a kiss.
When I lay down the good
deuce, he smacks his furrowed
brow and curses high heaven.

POOLSIDE

There is less than one hour left
and my father does not know.
He lies there in faded light
green trunks, turned belly-up
beneath a livid sunlamp,
smoking down his last cigar
before the time comes
for him to rise and dress.
He loves the sheer arrogance
of such heat, its dragon's
breath across his chest,
and he fills his lungs with it.

Minutes remain but still
he does not know. He thinks
of the long morning spent
riding bridle paths on a bay
gelding, the mid-day nap,
pinochle on a sun-drenched
patio and whiskey as clouds
turned his bright day dark
in the blink of an eye.
He thinks of tomorrow only
as a long drive home.

Seconds more as he rises
to stretch and blink salt
from his eyes. He does not
know yet. Without the least
thought of time winding down,
he tucks glasses in a towel
on the lounger and strides
across the deck as though

it were nothing. He breathes,
flexes his toes over the edge,
dives into the cool embrace
of deep water and dies.

KANSAS, 1973

My daughter nestled in a plastic seat
is nodding beside me as though in full
agreement with the logic of her dream.
I am glad for her sake the road is straight.
But the dark shimmer of a summer road
where hope and disappointment repeat
themselves all across Kansas like a dull
chorus makes the westward journey seem
itself a dream. She breathes in one great
gulp, taking deep the blazing air, and stops
my heart until she sighs the breath away.
The sun is stuck directly overhead.

I thought it all would never end. The drive,
the heat, my child beside me, the bright day
itself, that fathering time in my life.
We were going nowhere and never would,
as in a dream, or in the space between
time and memory. I saw nothing but sky
beyond the horizon of still treetops
and nothing changing down the road ahead.

DIALYSIS

In my brother's blind and dying
eyes I was forever young.
He rocked and slept to the sound
of my voice as long as memory
played its tune. Then he woke
to speak of vast silver platters
heaped with meat and bouquets
of cheese, hot loaves the way
we found them on the island.
He said my breath had carried
the dream along. We were back
to back again in the Valiant's
front seat, doors gaping and feet
on the seething summer streets
of Flatbush. As his eyes closed
and sullied blood spun in loops
of plastic tubing, I watched
my brother closing down his life.
Time dissolved in his mind,
leaving nowhere but the past
for him to live. His will to sit
through this ritual cleansing
weakened as each day blended
until only sleep remained.

THE FLASK

Behind glass in my daughter's dining room,
the cracked leather flaps of my father's flask
dangled from its shoulders like unfastened
suspenders. By candlelight I saw the oval
sixty-year old stain still centered on its plaid
coat in the place where a heart would be.
As we passed, hands filled with steaming bowls
of *Tortellini in Brodo,* the dented metal cap
my father used to measure shots of rye held
our faces for an instant like flashes of memory.

Now I am the child and he is alive. It is another
November night, his face grim in the glass
as he ties and reties his Windsor knot, bracing
himself with a swig from the flask for the dark
task ahead. In a blink of the eye we are inside
a dining room, strange people passing behind
me, smiling as they speak of my father's Kosher
chicken market, now theirs, and I watch hands
filled with steaming bowls of *Tortellini in Brodo*
set them down so that the scent fills my head
and lifts me into the autumn sky until nothing

made sense for a moment except my daughter
as she sat across from me, smiling at her groom,
turning to smile at me, her face slowly masked
by the steam that rose like the past made whole.

HERITAGE

These pink pills I hold in my palm
might have saved my father's life.

Insubstantial as tears, dust of fungus
pressed and formed into small shields,

they would have kept his heart open
for years to a full flow of blood.

But he felt nothing that said danger
hid in the mass of his chambers

and valves, so he did nothing but live
as his own father had lived and died.

Now I take one each night before sleep.
In the last week he has been returning

to me in dreams, always moving away
from the light, as though my reaching

the age he was at death freed him
at last to seek a final place of rest.

BREATH

For depth of breath young Sinatra
like a boxer ran five morning miles.
Solo on the high school track, thin
as the stripe on a lane, he was all
ears, all bone. He was all business.

The first laps were always for love
songs, nice and easy till he found
his rhythm, drawing the urban air
in deep. The moment he became
one with wind, he knew the way
a body held in check could move
exactly like a melody. It was simple
as swimming underwater. His stride
grew smooth, fingers to shoulders
to hips to toes, graceful as a smile
across low notes as the key shifted.

That was for the long lines of lyric
no one else could hold. In time he ran
for the uptempo tunes, let go a little
to get the torso involved and bring
his thin arms into play, his gait all glissando.
Step by step he swelled from the inside
out, making himself strong enough
for song. He ran past pain, timed by
the beat of his heart because song
was not about how fast but how long.
This was his Golden Age, Jersey City
in the early Thirties, his moment to make
dreams come true. Music was in the air.
He knew he could go on like that forever
because his dreams began with breath.

O'CONNOR AT ANDALUSIA

*Sickness before death is a very appropriate thing and I think those who
don't have it miss one of God's mercies.*
—Flannery O'Connor, *The Habit of Being*

It came with the steady pace of dusk,
slow shadings in the distance, a sense of light
growing soft at the center of her body.
It came like evening to the farm
bearing silence and a promise of rest.
There was nothing to say it was there
till she found herself unable to move
and stillness settled its net over the bed.
A crimson disc of pain suddenly flushed
from her hips like a last flaring of sun.

She believed the time had come
to embrace this perfect weakness
that had no memory of strength,
a mercy even as darkness hardened
inside her joints. It was not to be
missed. Nor was the mercy of sight:
she believed the time had come
to measure every moment and map
the place she soon must leave.
At least she had been given time,
though her wish would have been
an hour more for each leaf visible
from her window, a day for trees,
a week for birds and month to savor
the voice of each friend who called.
Though she never belonged in the heart
of this world, she gave this world her heart.

Within her stillness she remembered
the first signs: that brilliant butterfly
rash on her face, a blink that lasted
for hours, the delicate embrace of sleep
veering as in a dream toward the grip
of death, hunger vanishing like hope.
Her body no longer knew her body as itself

but this too was a mercy. To leave herself
behind and then return was instructive.
To wax and wane, to live beyond
the body and know what that was like,
a gift from God, a mixed blessing shrouded
in the common cloth of loss. Half her life
she practiced death and resurrection.

WHITMAN PINCH HITS, 1861

After six months of wandering Whitman found himself
at the edge of a Long Island potato farm in early fall.
He saw a squad of young men at sport on sparse grass.
Looking up, he saw a few stray geese rise and circle back
north as though confused by the sudden Indian summer,
then looked down to study cart tracks cut deep into mud.
Weary of his own company, shorn of appetite, he thought
it would be sweet to sit awhile beside this field and watch
the boys in their shabby flannel uniforms playing ball.
Caught between wanting to look at them and wanting
them to look at him, he could not tell from this distance
if the torn and faded blues they wore were soldiers' clothes
or baseball clothes. But he loved the rakish tilt of their caps
and cocky chatter drifting on the mid-day air. He had seen
the game played before, in Brooklyn, on a pebbled patch
laid out beside the sea, and thought it something young,
something brotherly for the frisky young and their brothers
to do in the shadow of civil war. That seemed two lifetimes
ago, not two years. The face he could no longer bear to find
in a mirror looked now like this island's ploughed ground.
Time does turn thick, Whitman thought, does press itself
against a man's body as he moves through a world torn apart
by artillery fire and weeping. Without knowing it happened,

he settled on a rise behind the makeshift home, moving
as he moved all year, a ghost in his own life. He should write
about baseball for the Eagle, or better still, make an epic poem
of it. The diamond chalked on grass, stillness held in a steady
light before the burst of movement, boys with their faces open
to the sky as a struck ball rose toward the all-consuming clouds.
But it was the sound that held him rapt. Wild, musical voices
punctuated by a pock of bat on ball, then the dropped wood
clattering to earth, grunts, everyone in motion through the air,

the resistant air, and then the lovely laughter. Whitman laughed
with them, a soundless gurgle. The next batter staggered and fell,
drunk, his chin tobacco-splattered, laughing at his own antics
as he limped back to the felled tree where teammates sat.
They shook their heads, ignoring the turned ankle he exposed
for them to admire. Suddenly all eyes turned toward Whitman

where he lounged, propped on one elbow, straw hat tilted
to keep the sun from his neck, on the hill that let him see
everything at once. They beckoned. They needed Whitman
to pinch hit, to keep the game going into its final inning.
The injured batter held his stick out, thick end gripped in his fist,
and barked a curse. Whitman sat up, the watcher summoned
into a scene he has forgotten he did not create. They beckoned
and he came toward them like a bather moving through
thigh-high breakers, time stopping and then turning back,
letting him loose at last amid the spirits that greeted him
as the boys pounded his back, as they turned him around
and shoved him toward the field. In his hands, the wood
felt light. He stood beside the folded coat that represented
home, shifted his weight and stared at the pitcher who glared
back, squinting against the sun, taking the poet's measure.

RAOUL DUFY AT FENWAY PARK, 1950

I. *The Letter*

Dr. Homburger at his desk in Boston
rocks in place and feels the cool face
of a stethoscope tapping his chest.
He gazes down at a magazine photo
in which Raoul Dufy sits at his tilted
desk in Montmartre. All Homburger
can see is the painter's warped hand
like a claw grappling his narrow brush.

The light is bad, but he knows the art
well enough to have noticed Dufy's
giddy flowers shrinking on their stems
year by year. Now he sees those hands
have been blooming with pain as well.

He looks away, allows a brief distraction
as morning sunlight winks off a sculler's
gleaming oars. Some days Homburger
would trade all he owns to see water
shimmer as Dufy has seen it, or feel
the depth of such blue as it ranges
through to joy. But then to lose all that!

The way Dufy's bouquets once burst
into smile. That implication of breeze
where threshers labored as a storm
gathered, or the lazy curves of a violin
at rest upon a rococo yellow console.
Homburger pushes aside the magazine
and centers a sheet of paper on his blotter.
He gathers himself and writes: *My Dear Dufy.*

II. *The Treatment*

Homburger thinks Dufy cannot be this
old man setting crutches aside as he sits
where afternoon light cannot reach.
He finally understands those stark black
paintings Dufy has done of late, men
frozen in place while a bull gathers strength,
figures etched against a sky dark enough
to stop the heart. The men have talked all
day, a collage of languages saying *hope*
and *help* till nothing remains but this
lifted syringe. For one instant, it points
toward skies that are a color Dufy has never
encountered before, then lets loose a drip
he sees as pure faith. It enters skin that
always feels afire. There is only more pain.

Dufy has not wanted to hear the name
of these new hormones, placing a tumid
finger across the doctor's lips whenever
Homburger speaks of them. *Cortisone.*
ACTH. No, he wants to feel their colors
rush, if he can, and looks away to find again
the memory of young sunbathers lounging
on pink and saffron blankets by the Charles.

III. *The Game*

Dufy crosses his room the way he imagines
snowmelt crosses rocks where a river is born.
He flicks a sable brush against his open palm
and looks through a stack of quick sketches,
flowers that bloomed as his fingers shrank
almost before his eyes. Within three days
he has gotten back his hands. The knock

of knuckles on his door like a throat clearing,
then Homburger is beside him at the open
window asking if there is anything he wants.

Twilight softens the air. The harbor waits
with arms open. *What more is there?*
In reply, the doctor fans a pair of tickets
to the Red Sox game and offers a royal
blue hat crowned with the team's red B.

Under the lights, Dufy is dazzled as much
by being able to climb steps and hold
a hot dog in his hand as by the delicate
dance of Dom DiMaggio under a fly
to deep centerfield. A woman seated
before Dufy wears a red rose in her hair
and drinks beer the color of summer

light above the harbor at Deauville.
Even the names afloat on the night
are blessings to his ear: *Dropo, Zarilla.*
When the crowd rises for a Williams
line drive, Dufy is up with them, laughing,
clapping his hands as the sound spirals
like a spray of anemones from their vase.

LOST PSALM

God was the clear pane at the heart
of a stained glass burning bush
filling the temple's western wall.

God was water when I walked
the beach during the eye
of a hurricane. God was water
swelling as the storm moved
across land and then was
the storm in full force.
God was a dune risen
to meet the surge and God
was a dune shrunk
to welcome winter wind.

God was on the tongue
of the first girl I kissed,
then God was on my tongue.

God spoke with flickering
light in a flood of sighs,
spoke without breath,
warm, spoke in tongues.

God was high in the stands
when I was knocked free
of time and space for one
full week making a tackle
in the open field. I shook
on the ground as if charged
by His light. All next spring
and early summer, God sped

through cycles of color
just beyond the edge of sight.

Doctors named it an aftereffect
of trauma but I understood it
was the afterglow of grace
and for months God could be
glimpsed in the creases of dream,
heard just beyond the bell buoy

at land's end, felt in spindrift
when the moon was full.

Finally God was in eastern
Pennsylvania, looming in books
and seminars. But somewhere
on the Susquehanna near Safe Harbor,
crewing a Flying Dutchman,
stretched out to my fullest
over the rushing river
in an effort to keep us all afloat,
I lost Him in a sudden luff of wind.

LATIN LESSONS

The daughter of the local florist taught
us Latin in the seventh grade. We sat
like hothouse flowers nodding in a mist
of conjugations, declining nouns that
made little sense and adjectives that missed
the point. She was elegant, shapely, taut.
She was dazzling and classic, a perfect
example to us of such absolute
adjectives as *quite* or *too* or *perfect.*
The room held light. Suffering from acute
puberty, we could still learn case by case
to translate with her from the ancient tongue
by looking past her body to the chaste
scribblings she left on the board. We were young
but knew that the ablative absolute
was not the last word in being a part
of something while feeling ourselves apart
from everything that mattered most. We chased
each other on the ballfield after class
though it did no good. What we caught was not
what we were after, no matter how fast
we ran. She first got sick in early fall.
A change in her voice, a flicker of pain
across her face, and nothing was the same.
She came back to us pale and more slender
than ever, a phantom orchid in strong
wind, correcting our pronoun and gender
agreement, verb tense, going over all
we had forgotten while she was gone. Long
before she left for good in early spring,
she made sure the dead language would remain
alive inside us like a buried spring.

NIGHT WIND

I woke to wind that rose
from far below the dawn.
It spoke of light as lost
for good, as dream only,
then died. Creeping thyme
ruffled the window screen,
letting its scent loose
in our room, lacing the air
with a deep taste of green.

If there were the bluebird's
soft flutings or scrub jay's
notes, I would have turned
myself over to the morning.
But all I heard were screech
owls' crazed whistles
that meant night was holding.
I felt time stretch and curl
itself back into the distance
from which wind rose again.

THE END OF DREAMS

He wakens knowing this to be the day
his hopeless singing voice at last will sound
exactly like the young Robert Goulet.
It is the day for him to touch the ground
as only noble Fred Astaire has done
before, and only once, and with someone

perfect in his arms. He will be able
to accompany himself on the grand
piano by sight, bass hand and treble
hand like swallows in flight, each magic hand
nimble and light as the air that trembles
with the music he will make at the end

of all his dreams. It feels simple and right
to draw in all the air he can, to grow
still, then soar. Now they all stand around
his bed, in tears, and he sees the pure light
that means the time has come for him to sound
the first note, take the first step, and let go.

ELIOT IN THE AFTERNOON

In the fourth year of drought,
in late September when our parched garden
was lost to spotted spurge and blackberry vine,
when only Russian sage and flannel bush thrived
in their tonsure of blonde grass near our bedroom
window and the fig stood cockeyed with heat,

I sat in a cracked Adirondack chair under twin fir,
occupying the daily zone between analgesic doses,
watching bees traffic around wild rosemary

and saw out of the corner of my eye Eliot show
himself beside our slowly dying well.
                                        At first
he was pooled light that burst into flame
and became a flare of wind-blown leaves
as I turned to look.
                    Though this light was soaked
up at once by swaying oak and box elder, I had time
to think: You won't need that umbrella here.

I did not remember seeing hallucinations
listed as a side effect of this drug, and with all signs
of him vanished I sat back to catch the frozen
dance of a rufous hummingbird above yarrow.

Then I noticed Eliot's bowler nestled in a fold
of land where we stacked deadfall for winter fires.
I stood, shading my eyes, and saw the hat
for what it was: a dented boulder half-emerged
from its niche, our customary seat at the nightly
Concerto for Water Dripping Into Near-Empty Tank,
in the key of Despair Minor.

He remained beyond reach,
a shape without mass in the space between trees,
but I knew he had come. All day, to pass the time,
I had been trying to reconcile the cycles
of my illness with the cycles of rainfall, the rise
and fall of temperature or barometer, phases
of moon, patterns of cloud. It seemed fit
that out of such fruitless brooding Eliot should
arrive, accompanied by the warbler's *twit twit twit,*
and decide not to *come too close.*

                                           I believed it
best to be still, as with a spooked cat, and let
him join all us *creatures of the summer heat.*

Should I call him Tom or Mr. Eliot?
Should I ask him to sit with me in the shade?
Should I offer him a peach?

I must have slept, because sky was going silver
with vague cirrus when I saw him move across
the gravel drive. He had found a deer trail
that drops toward the creek dry since April
of 1995. But instead of descending, he floated
among the trees as though transformed
to warm breeze.
                      Then he was beside me.

I thought of all the things to avoid mentioning:
the state of poetry today, the fact that I am a Jew,
the mess virus has made of my body or how far
we are from the city. He was *an old man*
and this was *a dry month,* season, year....
Best, I thought, not to quote him.
Even better not to amend his lines.

Mr. Eliot, we need to find the deep aquifer.

Especially at summer dusk, we have been lulled by
voices singing out of empty cisterns and exhausted wells.
Lulled by late darkness and the hope of deep mountain
snows next winter, dreams of extravagant melts
next spring followed by long rains that linger
at least through July. Now it is too late, the well
has all but died, *only rock and no water*
and the gravel road.
                                   Who better to remind us
that the time has come to drill deep, to trace
the remote history of water down so that *time future*
does not *contain time present.*
                                   I meant so that cycles
cease to matter because we find ourselves down
where water always flows, the realm of ancient
floodwater freeing us from the desiccated surface
and its arid shallow layers.
                                   Tom, we need a new well
and they charge by the foot!
                                   For the first time
he turned to smile, the London banker knowing a sound
investment when he heard it. Before I could speak,
he was back where the pooled light had blazed,
afloat as though sailing on a hidden sea. He knew
his way around a small craft and the wind.
He knew his way home without markers.

Soon he began to fade. Or perhaps it was a trick
of light in air too sere to hold him there,
or the presence of my wife, mugs of tea in hand,
smiling at me in a way he only remembered
from late in his life, that second chance at love.

Polite as ever, he took himself to the edge
of the hill, looking down, looking away
over the valley shadowed now by evergreen,
showing me the light, a shimmering vision
that may have been water, and drifted off.

DOWSING FOR JOY

The dowser says he can discover joy
as well as water or the whereabouts
of elk in hunting season. Unfurled wire
hangers and forked sticks nestle in a leather
quiver he carries up our gravel drive
until a fold of land calls him to the west.

In the woods he seems half his eighty years
and his pale blue eyes deepen to sapphire
as he gazes where the breeze disappears.
He says there are signs everywhere,
obvious things that most of us simply miss
like the scent of blooming lilies carried on air,
or hidden fields of force that call us home
when we can no longer bear to be alone.
What is music but waves plucked from the sky
and is color not light disturbed before the eye
can find it ? He reminds us no one doubts
the fact that wild animals know weather
well enough to hide before a storm arrives.
Are we not animals too? The agitation of a boy
lost in the forest pulls like the moon on tides
if a dowser is tuned in, if he can ask
the right question at the right time and cast
his spirit before him into the dark.

He stops to stake a vein of water for the site
of our well and strings ribbon over limbs
to track its turnings. Something tells him
there is more to know here. Among the oak
and fir he whispers questions to the night
ahead and smiles first at me, then at my wife
as the wires in his fists cross to find us both.

NABOKOV, MIST

My mind has made colossal efforts to distinguish the faintest of personal
glimmers in the impersonal darkness on both sides of my life.
–Vladimir Nabokov, *Speak, Memory*

At first I thought it was an elk,
only the antlers visible above
morning mist, moving in waltz
time as in a dream. Though it was
bodiless, I knew in the fluid
landscape of long-term illness
nothing was impossible. Not even
the late season butterflies I saw next,
Pine Whites like supple tendrils
of flaring mist torn loose to quiver
in a sudden crosswind.

Then the elk shedding mist
revealed itself as Nabokov,
heavy as in his *Lolita* years,
net raised, eager for one more capture.

I saw nothing could distract him
from his prey. He moved without
motion and in the shifting haze
was pure consciousness within
a twist of shadow, drifting due north.

He always meant to explore this far
into Oregon, following the movement
of blues across one more summer.
In June when I saw a male Spring Azure
pale among our blueberry bushes,
I thought of Nabokov coming to life
at the very sight. The same day,
my cane sunk in mud, I saw

a Common Blue settle on silky lupine
in the meadow and sensed a ghost
of silvery flight against the hill's fold.

But till now I could not allow myself
to believe Nabokov was here,
collecting specimens, fading in
and out of sight. Yet here
he was, an example of slow
adaptation to death, perhaps,
or miracle of the mind's endless life.
A leak of light from the deep
dark he never wished to accept,
Nabokov winks with his whole body.

As I watch him circle the cosmos,
the mist begins to lift. He does not
see me, but in the clarifying light
I understand that he notices everything
else. Yarrow ruffled by his passing.
A rufous hummingbird frenzied
and hovering before the purple foxglove,
yellow umbels of fennel feathering
as wind begins to rise, Sara Orangetips
bouncing in a sun-drenched cluster
of mustard. I wonder if these were
there before Nabokov saw them for me.
Yes his body says as it opens to emit
a streak of sun. *This is heaven.*

He leaves behind a tinge
of Russian sage, something blue
across the grass like a silhouette
of laughter. As though fresh
from the land without seasons,
a Red Admiral circles the last place
Nabokov appeared, its wings wide
against the memory of mist.

V *from* Approximately Paradise

THE ROLE OF A LIFETIME

I am bound upon a wheel of fire
—King Lear

He could not imagine himself as Lear.
He could do age. He could rage on a heath.
Wounded pride, a man gone wild: he could be clear
on those, stalking the stage, ranting beneath
a moon tinged red. Let words rather than full
throated roars carry fury while the wind
howled. He could do that. And the awful pull
of the lost daughter, the old man more sinned
against than sinning. The whole wheel of fire
thing. But not play a wayward mind! Be cut
to the brains, strange to himself, his entire
soul wrenched free, then remember his lines but
act forgetting. Understand pure nonsense
well enough to make no sense when saying
it. Wits turned was one thing; wits in absence
performed with wit was something else. Playing
Lear would force him to inhabit his fear,
fathom the future he had almost reached
already. Why, just last week, running here
and there to find lost keys, a friend's name leached
from memory. Gone. No, nor could he bring
himself to speak the plain and awful line
that shows the man within the shattered king:
I fear I am not in my perfect mind.

GAUGUIN IN OREGON

In relapse again, I have been dreaming
of my body buried in white blossoms
that flutter from the bitter cherry,

soft as the spring breeze and scent
of hyacinth wafting through the screen,
accompanied by a sound like the strokes
of a brush on canvas .

                         An owl?
Deer browsing the hillside trails.
No, the winter creek still surging.

I think I am awake now.

                         Between rains,
finespun mist drifts among the oak
and swaying fir, a ballet choreographed
in dreamtime, costumed in black
and gray. The music, I realize, is made
from shades of dawn, is all cloud,
delicate as the creamy crown
of an early daffodil.

                         My eyes close again,

but then I see him move.

                         Gauguin!
I would know him anywhere. My size,
my age, but looking fresh from a wrestle
with angels. I was reading about him
only yesterday.

                         Saffron-colored shirt
like a glimpse of sun, fringe of hair tangling
where I thought to see leaves, bandy legs
unsteady on the sloping land, he reaches

as if grasping one last fruit of the dark.
Where his stained hands slash through a web
of clouds, colors bleed together, stars vanish.

He radiates rage. I sit up against the headboard,
blinking, naked in a snarl of white sheets.
I know I am awake now.
                                        His form tells me
Gauguin expects to find himself again
in an island paradise. The sort of place,
he wrote, where *Life is singing and loving*.
The afterlife as advertised to the child
he was in Peru, as dreamed by the seaman
he became in the frozen north, as sketched
by the heartsick wild-man dying on Dominique.
A century dead, he must be more sensitive
to cold than ever. Surely he knows by now
that paradise is approximate.
                                        Though he lusts
for heat and seething tropical morning light,
here those vapors dancing before his eyes
will have to do. He stalks his way east
toward the crest, lush with Turk's lily
and wild iris. Their sudden color stops him.

Gauguin, if I am not mistaken, is hearing
inner music, a vibration of blues and golds,
the pure vermilion resonance he remembers
as the color a cello turns when played
in its deepest register. I see the savage
glee in his eyes as he looks around,
forgetting where he is in time
to find the lone lilac about to bloom.
Thirst stirs in him. Hunger.
                                        He died
at fifty-five, dreaming of food and wine,

and I am fifty-five, dreaming of burial
by fruit trees that bear no fruit.
Lost in time, back in bed since the dead
of winter, I have woken in the dark
in absolute certainty that it was seven
years ago. Then, in a heartbeat, five
years from now.
                    I must walk to Gauguin
before he vanishes. Against a hazing sky,
he is already growing light and I go out
where the morning colors gather.

CARSON McCULLERS AT THE SPINET

Against New York winter light, the hiss
of passing tires and rants of New Year's drunks,
her Chopin nocturnes always conjured
Georgia nights with Mama and Brother-Man.
Cream sherry tinted gold by candleflame.
Plates of steamed artichokes and clarified
butter in etched cups, their scents mingling
with a languid Chattahoochee River breeze,
toothpicks jutting from the cubed hearts.
Moody bird-chatter under the melody line.
Smoke in the air and the breath of family
everywhere. She could make the harsh
northern seasons flow without notice
over the stones of time, her music slow
and sultry while crisp darkness took hold.

Now, after three strokes, she is only cold.
She sits at the spinet, the stiffened claw
of her left hand folded deep in her lap.
Straight ghostly fingers flash across
cracked keys, still sharp in the upper
register, and she hears the familiar melodies,
but none of it is real. Her good eye
sees the shadowy silhouette of a Christmas
tree flicker in a draft near the window.
Frost flowers on the panes. When no one
else is there, she will unfurl her fist and dare
the simple left-hand of a Scarlatti sonata.
She will seek a Schubert song, her strong
soprano voice flooding the lost notes.

BRAHMS IN DELIRIUM

–Vienna, 1890

He hears the sound of sunset as a cello
and snowflakes as flutes above a soft wind
of clarinets. All the reds and yellows
of a fall afternoon are oboes in his mind.

He knows he is out of his mind. He hears
the swift percussion of his racing heart
and feels it carry him toward what he fears
most, the end of all his music, the start

of everlasting silence. Faint harp notes
burst to the surface of each breath. He strips
to the waist, crosses the room. His face floats
in the washstand's mirror and water drips

down his flushed cheeks, his beard. He sees
an overturned jug hover above his head.
Now all it holds are a few melodies,
a passage in strings for all the unsaid

words, a theme shredded like winter light
as the snow ceases to fall. Then, nothing.
Silence will at last fill the room, and night
come on with its own secret songs to sing.

FRANÇOIS COUPERIN'S SECRET HARPSICHORD

–Paris, 1732

In the room beyond the room
where Couperin composed suites
for roving shadows and butterflies,

in the time after music
stopped for good and his heart grew
thick with trapped rhythms,

in darkness lit only by a trio of tapers
Couperin conjured his perfect harpsichord.

Its case was shaped like the wings
of angels, but lean and flowing
as though honed for long flight.

Made of poplar brushed to the luster
of cypress, the body would glow
with all he remembered of dawns
spent composing at his sycamore desk,

of Paris streets in moonlight, or the vast
breath filling a young bagpiper's chest.

He would test each iron wire string,
match each slip of wood to its proper
quilled tip. Eyes closed, hands poised,
he imagined each plucked tone living
to linger on the air, resisting decay.

That should be the sound heard in heaven.

Some days his lungs seemed to fill

the room with their yearning and all
he could do was rest. He heard
above the frightened linnet of his wheezing
the sound light would make
if only it could find its way into music.

Those days, knowing himself to be
deep in the brief coda of his years,
Couperin saw himself painting
the thinnest gold leaf band on the lid,
testing the joints of the wrestplank
papering the smoothed interior
as a blossoming orchard where songbirds
thrived. One night he would paint a breeze.
One night the melody of the Seine.

He would give days to the bone and black
oak keyboard. Down on the floor
with parchment and veneer, he would shape
a rose for the hole in its flowered soundboard.

All would be balance. All would be clean
and dry. He never knew how much longer
to worry about the color of sound,
the poise of touch. But near the end,
as his fevers rose, he dreamed in counterpoint,
seeing four sets of hands move across
the upper manual, all his, all longer
and wiser than at any time in his life.

SOFT FLAME

He recognizes no one in his dreams.
The brother is not his brother, the child
not his child. His wife, all amber light, streams
through a window that is not there. A wild
current of wind warms the night and he sees
he is no longer himself either. June,
bitter cherry blossoms drift from the trees
to form clouds that slowly cover the moon,

and somewhere he can hear himself calling
in a voice that is not his voice. His name
fills the night, rising with light and falling
around him like the blanket of soft flame
that is his wife whispering him awake,
beckoning him to the brink of daybreak.

DRESS REHEARSAL

His second act costume weighs fifteen pounds,
and he must dance in it under hot lights
while singing with an alto whose voice sounds
like a full moon blazing on summer nights.

Smiling all the while, he must project ease,
the wit of a rogue prince whose true passion
is for battle, and grace enough to please
this young partner. But his face is ashen,

brow drenched. Breath is elusive as the birds
he tries to describe in this endless song.
He stops. If he could recall the rhymed words
that take him offstage now, he would be gone

for good. Nothing comes to him. There are wings
everywhere, action shattering the still
moment he hoped to create. Hazy rings
of light, behind which an audience will

be applauding at this time tomorrow,
fade as he awaits the falling curtain
now, lost in a soft, rapturous sorrow
where nothing moves and nothing is certain.

YESHIVA IN THE PALE, JANUARY, 1892

Early morning, as Cossacks on horseback
circled the old wooden synagogue, chants
seeped out like smoke through the walls. Black
hatted elders inside shut their eyes and danced
in circles of their own before the holy ark
Prayer deepened the air as one fat soldier nailed
the Tsar's seal to the door: CLOSED. Then a spark
cast from somewhere near the rising sun sailed
across the wintry sky, encircling soldier
and temple, nuzzling rooftree, gable, beam.
It found the place where mingled rage and dream
were draft enough to let a wildfire smolder.
One moment shadows questioned the winter dark
and next moment the answer arrived in flame.

THOMAS HARDY AT BOCKHAMPTON

At birth the doctor gave him up for dead,
setting him on the hearthstone. But the nurse
saw breath. It was a sudden blaze of spirit, she said,
more light than air. She knew he was its source

and snatched him up as the room filled with cold
fire. She felt in her bones he would be old
before his time, saw him haunted by strange
shapes, darkness within the avid dance of flame.

She watched him grow as though penned in a cage.
His hopes tangled in shadow by the back
door, their loss tinged with the scent of lilac.
Then woodland and sullen heath became

his heart's home. Bent oak, furze, a rose's thorn
would always mean the place where he was born.

JAMES McNEILL WHISTLER AT ST. IVES

−Cornwall, 1883

Whistler needs no one to sit for him now.
He is finished with portraits, with people.
Finished with nocturnes too, soft edges,
the muted light of a coastal fogscape.
He needs surprise. He wants to be outside
with a panel of wood, a thumb box of colors
and brushes, and nothing to hold him in place.
Bring on the war of sea and shore, clouds
blown apart. Autumn daylight like a shock
to the heart stirs him to life. He is after
the spontaneity of a breaker turned back
on itself. What is a whitecap but a stroke
of wind on wave, the Lord's own breath
in a flash of foam? Away too long from storm,
from the sea's surge, he feels himself awaken
before the horizon's shifting form, where time
itself is visible to the naked eye, where a ship
caught in a trough struggles to right itself.

JOHN CONSTABLE AT SIXTY

–London, 1837

Alone in the city, alone with memories
of Maria and their home on the heath,
Constable closes his eyes to find the sky
very close to his heart now. If he could
paint what he has come to know of it,
he would leave out the high blues,
leave out the watery violet that daylight
makes of a late winter afternoon
and the sea's azure embrace on clear
summer days. There will be no more
of these for him. He would rely on reds
now, the heavenly blood that warns
of storms, the blush rushing west
to east from the depths of a hidden sun.
His heart's hue. He would turn to reds
for their tint of certain loss on a day
otherwise full of promise, the hard truth
he learned from his wife's glazing eyes.
He would turn away from the comfort
of graying cumulus, the flicker of shadow.
It is his pleasure to imagine himself at last
one with the sky. But he will paint nothing
again, feels nothing calling him out
of his swollen heart. In the city, he feels
so much older than his years, as though aging
two for every one Maria has been gone.
What he remembers is that it took so long
for him to look up from the landscape,
to forget those paired swans on the lake
at Wivenhoe Park, scattered cattle at pasture,
visible dew and breeze, wildflowers in bloom
along a fold of hill, the distant copse,
the mill, the sprawling manor house.

But once he saw the sky for what it was,
the sky was all he could see. It was the spirit's
true shade, the Lord's lyric cry a man alone
heard and never forgot. Till now. The sky
is gone from his sight, taken into his body,
and all that remains is in tatters above
the city's dark buildings as he walks,
lost in thought, always looking down.

HOME REPAIRS

The summer he wallpapered his daughter's
bedroom, rain finally buckled the back deck
and sluiced the loose roof shingles free to
flutter off on a gust of wind. He knew
what was happening before his eyes, how water
goes for what holds an old house together
and tears it apart from the outside in.
So does the sun. A week of record heat
seemed to draw the house in upon itself
as he steamed, peeled and scraped through sheet
after sheet of tulips, roses, toy soldiers
and prancing horses. He could hear the thin
cry joists make as they dry. He worked by himself,
a storm of plaster around his shoulders,
the air thick with mold and age, nothing left
to mark the past but bare wall, a tapestry
of cracks, and a door that would not stay closed.

UNDER AN AUGUST MOON

This is the Green Corn Moon. This is the end
of summer rising with heat in its fat red fist.
Stars shoot through the night. The trend is
toward lingering high pressure off the coast.
By day, flat blue skies; by night, stillness
growing darker, denser. Power fails.
Mars has come near and looms to the south.
There is something starker than ever
to this August, an eloquence in its fever pitch.
Speech fails to convince. We want thunder
and heavy rain but get lightning strikes
and wildfires. The peace is broken,
deserts of the east in flames, the west
torrid with terror. Promise turns threat
and the heavens press upon us.
This is the error of our ways.
The corn crop stands scorched in its ears.
The sun saying we have learned nothing
will stare us down in the morning.

LUNCH IN THE ALZHEIMER'S SUITE

My mother smiles at me. She reaches out
to touch my face and wonders who I am.
The fleck of tuna dangling from her mouth
falls as she asks "Can you find me a man?"
Swaying willow and afternoon drizzle
fracture the light that falls across her tray.
Her hands, as though assembling the puzzle
lunch has become, adjust fork, bowl and plate,
adrift in shadows. Sometimes she forgets
to swallow. Sometimes she holds a spoonful
of soup in the air and loses herself
in its spiraling steam. In a whirlpool
of confusion she may suddenly sink
in her seat and chew nothing but thin air.
She is fading away. Her eyes grow dark
as she looks at the old man sitting there
claiming to be her son. She slowly shakes
her head, lifts an empty cup and drinks.

MIDNIGHT IN THE ALZHEIMER'S SUITE

Lost in the midnight stillness, my mother
rises to dress and begin another
chilly day. She crosses the moonlit floor.
There is too much silence beyond the door,
and a lack of good cheer, so she breaks
into song. But the coiling lyric snakes
back on itself and tangles in her throat.
She stops long enough to see a cloud float
along the hall, but somehow the cloud speaks
in the voice of the night nurse. Someone peeks
from a doorway. Now someone starts to moan,
someone else coughs and my mother's stray song
returns for a moment: *oh you belong
to me!* If the audience would quiet
down, she would remember. Opening night,
that's what this must be, and the curtain parts,
and the spotlight is on, the music starts,
but there is too much movement, too much noise,
yet she cannot stop, must maintain her poise,
smile and keep on singing. Then it must be
over because the night nurse is there, she
embraces my mother and leads her back
offstage, whispering, bringing down the dark
again. Tired, but pleased with her last set,
my mother lies down for a well-earned rest.

RELOCATION

Thirty thousand feet above the Badlands
my mother looks out her window and says
"There's a car beside us." She understands
for a moment that we are flying, prays

aloud for the pilot to find his way
through all this dark. Then she asks why
the chairs in our hotel are so small today.
She says there is something in my eye

and brushes her finger across the lid
of her own. Seeing the papery skin
loose on the back of her hand, its grid
of wrinkles, she blinks and asks again

how old she is. When I say she is ninety,
she looks away, sees the engine, turns
back and grabs my arm. She asks if I see
the car, then whispers that she yearns

to go upstairs to her room and invites
me to join her. There is nothing I can do
to help her through the long nights
ahead, nights strange as this afternoon

when we cross the country together.
Though she can no longer live alone,
I realize that no matter where my mother
lives now, she will always be alone

in a world forever gone wild in her mind.
Still thinking I am her last late boyfriend,
she leans closer, says "you're always so kind
to me" and sighs as she pats my hand.

SALMON RIVER ESTUARY

Drifting close to shore, we enter the shadow
of Cascade Head. Our kayak jitters in an eddy
as we dip and lift the double-bladed paddles
to keep ourselves steady. Lit by morning sun,
current and rising tide collide before our eyes
in swirls of foam where the river becomes
the sea. Surf seethes across a crescent of sand.
Gone now the bald eagle's scream as it leaves
a treetop aerie, the kingfisher's woody rattle,
gulls' cackle, wind's hiss through mossy brush.
Light flashing through sea mist forges a shaft
of color that arcs a moment toward the horizon
and is gone. Without speaking, moving together,
we power ourselves out of the calmer dark
and stroke hard for the water's bright center
where the spring tide will carry us back upriver.

STRIKING THE SET

After the last curtain falls
and the audience has gone
the actors drift back
onstage, dressed for the real
world again. They wander
the set, makeup caking necks,
an eye shadowed, a face
streaked with dark creases.

The young man who played
an aging bachelor still slouches
in character, his temples grayed
but a light now wild in his eyes.
The mail clerk/disgraced soldier
flashes a disposable camera
from the wings. The widow
and her tall killer husband
have hammers in their hands
and are smiling in a way
no one in the cast recognizes.

But everyone waits, some in tears,
others impatient to be gone.
A small chorus standing stage left
finally harmonizes on the lyric
blown tonight in Act Two.
From his seat in the back row,
the Director lifts his customary
closing night bottle of Bourbon,
freeing them to bring down
the world they made together.

HOMECOMING

The place he always hoped to live
waits just beyond this crest.
He knows he is close,
though a twist of cedar smoke
is all he can see of it.

Stopping to rest,
he lets a crust of soda bread
soften on his tongue
as he thinks
how all those wrong turnings
matter so much less
now that the end is in sight,
those nights alone
in cabins open to the skies,
that fraying rope
of muscle in his back,
the early pace
that could not have been held
by a man half his age,
a lack of water, a lack of light.

Up ahead the evergreen thin
and straggle, tips snagging
late afternoon mist.

The hour is lost
but at last he can see
where bare land begins
in a scatter of ancient till.

There among the cobbles
and boulders, in a flicker
of shadow over the saxifrage,

he knows nothing is left
but wind to contend with.

THE GEOLOGY OF HOME

We live on the limb of an overturned fold,
a shadow zone come late afternoon
when the crest is set ablaze. Just past
the hinge line wild blackberry thrives,
draping itself around a bed of stones.
Nothing is ever guaranteed here.
The compressed earth beneath our house
can heave and bend like a lamb at play,
young enough to change in a flash.
This morning, in a windless moment,
I saw stillness gather itself and abandon
first the grass, then the blotched iris,
tulips, fennel, twin oaks, feathery cirrus
and finally the faint crook of a quarter moon.

PATRICK KAVANAGH AT FIRST LIGHT

I am king/Of banks and stones and every blooming thing.
—Patrick Kavanagh, "Inniskeen Road: July Evening"

Through my bedroom window I see the old
man rise from his knees as though floating
on shadows. He comes and goes as I waken,
clear for a moment among the oak and pine,
then gone, then back where the bank folds
in a tangle of blackberry vines on the hillside.

His large hands sift a palmful of soil as he stares
into the distance and hears, I imagine, the call
of the dawn train headed south. This late
in July, morning climbs the horizon in fits
and starts. I turn over. From five miles away,
a car's headlights sweep the valley and flash
Kavanagh's hunched shadow against my wall.

Then I am beside him. The brim of a battered
fedora hides his eyes. As he brushes his hands
together, scattered dirt catches in the cuff
of his pants. He dislodges a rock from its niche
between us using the worn edge of his boot heel
and mutters *I see your land is only tumbled stones*
and a worrying wind. "Like Inniskeen," I tell him.
"So you should feel right at home here."

At that my wife stirs and sighs. So I have gone
nowhere after all, and realize I have been talking
to myself. Except there is Kavanagh again, quick
as a finch, perched atop an Adirondack chair
near the yarrow just coming into bloom.
He glares at daybreak's bittersweet glow
now seeping through the leaves and spreads

his arms. *A mile of kingdom,* he whispers
into the sudden breeze. I know there is nothing
he would not give for one more royal summer
in the country of light. Drifting back to sleep,
I hear him move cast through a break in the trees.

AMITY HILLS

I came here uneasy with the strange ways of forest life,
the crying sound of a white oak swaying in winter wind,
      mellow huff of deer settling to sleep
          on a slope, the soft rain–
      after sunset has spread like a stain–
becoming sudden storm rushing through the valley as night
falls, or the steady return of wildness across a thin
          margin we have made to keep
      ourselves still within the seasons' wax and wane.

And I was slow to fathom the loudmouth tree frogs' bright green
exuberance in underbrush as the pond rose with March
      runoff. Never knew what fog looked like
          from above, or how it seeped
      through leaves like the spirit of a breeze.
What dawnlight does to the dew trapped on a torn windowscreen.
I had not slept outdoors or lost myself under an arch
          of fir and climbed the hillside's
      contours home. I never felt as free

as the evening grosbeak bursting like flame from a snowdrift
in late November, as the maple trapped in its cycle
      of reddening but soon enough to
          begin budding. Life was slow
      to change here but change would go
on endlessly, and seldom seemed to change pace. Morning mist
sometimes formed itself into a blazing rainbowed circle
          above our house and would do
      a kind of dance before it was through

with us. I never knew how connected weather was to
the tint of leaf, or light was to where coyote crossed a hill,
      time was to the space a forest claimed

                    for deadfall. Till, near fifty,
          I finally left the city
and went to be with my love in her round house in the woods,
where soil was hard, water deep, and the late June air was cool.
          We live where nothing is tame,
          above a small town called Amity

at the stony end of an ancient lava flow, on massed
rock left by Ice Age floods. Poison oak and blackberry vines
          thrive here. By year's end a creek will rise
                    from the hill's heart and pour
          for six months upon the valley floor,
dwindling back underground when the summer solstice has passed.
Time here has drawn me out beyond strangeness. Or drawn me in.
          I have learned that surprise
          is not always shock and nothing to fear,

that the dark-eyed juncos throng when wild fennel goes to seed,
that Indian summer can color the landscape of dreams
          gold through a winter of freeze and thaw,
                    that the pattern of wind
          and the way old growth trees have been thinned
together help a harsh September rain carve itself deep
into the ridge exactly where evening sun always seems
                    to soften the least flaw
          in all we see before the dark begins.

REESE IN EVENING SHADOW

I prayed for easy grounders
when Pee Wee Reese fielded,
hanging curves when he hit.
At Ebbets Field, in late August
of my eighth year, I watched
him drift under a windblown
pop fly, moving from sunlight
to shadow as he drew near home.

Now, on the first anniversary
of his death, the August night
is wild with mosquitos and bats,
skunk in the compost. A pack of deer
thrashes through tangled hazel
and poison oak as they cross the hill
below its crest in search of water.

Nursing the day's final herbal
concoction against joint pain
and lost sleep, the same drink
I have used all twelve years
of my illness, I tilt my head back
in its battered Dodgers cap to rest
against the slats of an Adirondack chair

as a screech owl's solo whistle
pierces the endless crescendo
of bullfrogs and bumble bees

when Reese at last drifts back out
of evening shadows. He wears
loose flannels. Wrinkled with age,
stained by his long journey,

he still moves with that old grace
over the grass. I see anguish
of long illness on his familiar face
and something like relief too,
that rueful smile, the play finished,

game over. I stand and his arm
settles on my shoulder, a gesture
he used to silence the harrowing
of Jackie Robinson. He helps me
find balance while the world spins
as it always does when I rise
and the whisper of wind is his voice
saying it will be all right, pain is nothing,
stability is overrated, drugs play havoc
with your game, lost sleep only means
waking dreams, and illness is but a high
pop fly that pulls us into shadow.

He is gone as the wind he spoke with
dies down. I find myself on the trail
those deer walked, seeing where I am
now though already lost in a darkness
that soon will reach home.

WINTER SOLSTICE

I wake in darkness and fog to the hoofbeat of deer
racing across the hill's frosted crest from east to west.
As in a dream, within the rise and fall of wind I hear
the rise and fall of the deer pack's breath
as it becomes the beat of my heart within my chest.
I am fitted so close to my wife's body her breath
seems to be my breath as we curl together, awake
but not awake, her back rising against my rising chest
in the lingering pre-dawn dark.
Now, in the space between our breath, silence comes to rest.